Proven Pathways to Big Money Today

Proven Pathways to Big Money Today

An Idiot's Guide to Making Money Internationally

MAZHER H MALIK

Writers Club Press

San Jose New York Lincoln Shanghai

Proven Pathways to Big Money Today
An Idiot's Guide to Making Money Internationally

Writers Club Press
an imprint of iUniverse.com, Inc.

For information address:
iUniverse.com, Inc.
620 North 48th Street, Suite 201
Lincoln, NE 68504-3467
www.iuniverse.com

ISBN: 0-595-13041-0

Printed in the United States of America

NOTE

This publication is designed to express the Author's opinion only in regards to the subject matter covered. It is sold with the understanding that the Publisher or the Author is not engaged in rendering legal, accounting or other professional service.

If such assistance is required, the services of a competent professional person should be sought.

Whether you are poor or jobless
Sad or in a real financial mess
The Opportunities are plenty world wide
To be rich and happy follow this guide

CONTENTS

INTRODUCTION

Constant hardship can change some people's views about money and luck, and can force them to believe, that getting rich and enjoying a comfortable living was a prerogative of someone born lucky, or possessing very special skills. We are sure, they will start believing otherwise when they have finished reading this guide.

Money is important to everyone. It makes the world go round. Not having enough of it leads to frustration and a very dim view of life. Extreme poverty is a disaster; it can make a normal, intelligent person very mad, especially, if he has lot of commitments, or was buried deep in debt. It can upset his whole social balance, and destroy his health and peace of mind. It can even turn him into a criminal. The same could be true of a person having too much wealth: it can spoil him and make him indulge in excesses of all kinds, which can speed up his end. However, if wisely used, money can be a blessing.

Perhaps you are one who is looking for ways to make quick, regular cash without much fuss; or one, who is in search of ideas or opportunities for making real big money. The guide attempts to satisfy the needs of both. However, it will be of special interest to those who are not gainfully employed, and many others who, despite working hard, cannot make enough to lead a comfortable life. The idea is to develop a realistic and practical approach to increasing income by bringing opportunities into focus.

We are not endeavouring to propose quick, get-rich schemes, although you may well end up a millionaire, sooner than you could imagine, by following some of the ideas presented. Our aim is to point to the directions you should be heading, and the routes or the 'pathways' you should be following, in order to score high in the money-making game.

The first part of the book explains how ones thinking can give birth to an idea that can be turned into gold. It then goes on to show the nature of opportunities where and how they can be discovered and their relationship with TIME factor. The concept of LUCK is then discussed followed by the self-imposed constraints by many who work for others for a fixed pay, highlighting the contracting job market for many types of skills. The emphasis is laid on self-employment as the means to enormous wealth and how one can get assistance in that direction from various means and, how a proper action plan makes achievement of a goal very simple and possible.

The second part of the guide 'reveals' the actions or 'pathways' which can automatically lead one to ideas, opportunities and finally, to financial independence. The next part is a Case Book of Wealth Creators—people in real life, making it big.

The final part is devoted to some fast and easy ways of generating income ranging from a few dollars to a few millions, often from some simple ideas or business deals. Finally, in the appendices to the guide, comprehensive lists of business ideas and opportunities and useful contacts and information sources are given to trigger an action from the would-be wealth creator.

The predominant reason for producing this guide was to help ordinary people, especially those who are unemployed and desperate to find a source of income, to enable them to realise the potential merits of self-employment, i.e. having one's own business, rather than working for someone for a fixed pay. A person working for an employer is, effectively, a slave—he takes orders from his or her boss; on the other hand, the self-employed gives orders—to those whom he employs. Under the formal situation, the person has no control over his or her activity or time, while in the latter, the person has the control, and can do what he thinks is right; he can take a holiday whenever he or she feels like, can expand the business and income to suit his or her needs. The guide emphasizes the latter situation. It is the only way to big fortunes.

This doesn't mean one should leave one's job and go headlong into some business. And, also, it is important to understand, that a business does not always mean having an actual office, shop or factory. It could simply mean an activity, an idea or an arrangement which could bring one income. Many people make fortunes just from the comfort of their arm-chairs. Sounds incredible, but you will soon believe it once you have understood and appreciated the concepts explained herein, and especially, after reading the Case Book, supplementing this guide.

The Case Book, in fact, forms an important feature of this manual. It illustrates a number of true case studies—showing how ordinary people are getting rich everyday, many starting with little capital or knowledge of the business world. They show money-making in action. They also contain a wealth of factual information, and supplement the concepts illustrated in the earlier sections of the guide.

The guide has been written in a straightforward and simple style, without any jargons, so that any one with only basic knowledge can understand it.

It is also important to appreciate, that psychology plays a big role in what we wish to do or accomplish. There is often, for example, a tendency for someone to be suddenly inspired to achieve something, and then to forget all about it with the passage of time. The inspiration lasts for a few moments only. This should not happen if you really wish to succeed in your objective.

Your aim is to make money—BIG MONEY—because you know the comforts, happiness and the luxuries which money can bring. That is your goal. You must keep it ALIVE. To enable you to do that, we suggest that you read this guide a number of times. You will feel the difference it makes to your thinking, and eventually, to your life. It could lead you to riches, that is.

Mazherul H Malik
May 10, 2000

THINK MAN THINK !

The human brain is a powerful computer. It is more that. A man-made computer needs programming to operate, but the living brain does not. It programmes itself, as a person grows and becomes exposed to the world around him. The main, powerful function of the brain, is to think, and dictate the way a person should act or be have.

The thinking process of the brain is full of mysteries. It can be likened to a sort of energy, or rays of subtle, invisible light. When a person thinks, images are formed in his brain. The images can be compared with those formed on the retina of a human eye when a person is looking at an object. But in the latter case, the object is real and is physically present. In the former case, it may or may not be present.

You could also compare it with the tiny spots of light which form into a picture on a television screen. But again, there is a difference between a human brain and the television. The latter cannot think, but the former can.

Our thoughts dictate the way we should behave or act. If they are clear, then the images formed in our brain are also clear. Usually, images of something we are very much attached to emotionally, appear very clear.

The thinking process of the brain never ceases, unless one dies, or becomes unconscious. A person is always thinking of something: his work, his family, his loved ones, etc. In fact, the life itself is a series of thoughts. The thinking process may continue even when we are asleep, giving rise to images which appear very real. These are our dreams. When dreaming, we are in a different dimension, like we are when we are dead. But in the latter case, our physical connection with this world is severed; in the former it is not. The dreams are actually part of our physical life, because they tell us about our future. They are a sort of preview of what is going to happen to us, mentally and physically, in the not too distant future.

Since the whole thinking process dictates our life, then what we do, affects it. Clear, constructive thinking leads to success and greatness, while negative, confused thinking leads to failures and frustration. When our thinking is clear, then the brain concentrates and responds, by giving us guidance in the form of various suggestions. An IDEA, arising in our mind, is a suggestion from the brain, a sort of clue to something we must, or must not do; or the way a certain thing has to be done.

Our thoughts reflect our intentions. If they are clear, then what we intend to do is also clear. For example, when a person faces a problem, the thoughts will usually converge on that problem, giving rise to a suggestion or an idea, which, like a floodlight, illuminates the solution to the problem. Ideas are thus keys to successful resolution of our problems. They enable us to accomplish our aims in life.

Some people would often praise others for their success, but have very negative views of themselves—reflecting a rather passive way of thinking.

All human beings are bestowed with normal, thinking brain, but often, its power is dispersed and wasted. The reason is that ninety percent of human attention is taken up by many routine activities in his life. Worries, especially, take a big toll. A person could be worrying about his home, family or work. A single serious incident, a death of a loved one, for example, could grip his attention for days on end, never giving him chance to concentrate on things which were more important to his existence.

A positive attitude, therefore, needs to be developed. This helps to channel our physical and mental efforts towards attainment of our real objectives. It generates clear thinking and helps the brain to concentrate and generate ideas—ideas which offer solutions to our problems.

Ideas generate action. An action is, usually, the final product of the human thoughts. Clear, positive thoughts means clear, positive action. The thoughts, though are the driving force behind our intentions, they do not achieve anything on their own, because they are not something substance. Our action gives them substance.

To succeed in accomplishing a goal, therefore, clear thinking or concentration of mind is of paramount importance. It helps to programme one's intentions towards achieving that goal, resulting in the right action on one's part. A scientist thought of putting man on the moon. And he acted and did it. All famous writers, artists, poets and inventors were great thinkers, and thus, achieved great things.

If you wish to succeed in your life, think about the opportunities around you. THINK BIG. Visualise your goal. Think about it clearly and seriously. Think about it all the time. See it happening in front of your eyes. And it will actually HAPPEN.

The Nature of Opportunities

Money or wealth cannot be created unless there are opportunities which could be exploited.

Opportunities can either be recognised or created. One who recognises an opportunity, knows a lot about the money making game. One who creates it, is a born money maker; he knows it all and is a professional in the game.

For example, if while walking down a high street in a town, you happen to notice, that there was not a single fruit shop, then this presented an opportunity for a business which will generate income. If someone opened a fruit shop there, then that someone had recognised the opportunity, and, used it. The opportunity arose from a need. The need was for a basic food item—fruit. Wherever and whenever there is a need, there is an opportunity. The absence of a fruit shop presented an opportunity to satisfy a need. It just required someone to recognise it.

On the other hand, there are people who may not only recognise opportunities, they actually create them. People in this category educate others to think differently, by various persuasive ways. They bring a change in the society, especially, in the attitudes and life styles of people, and, in the process, create a lot of wealth for themselves.

Take Kellogg's Corn Flakes, for example. Corn is a simple food item, but Kelloggs made it into a nourishing breakfast cereal. By continuous advertising, they popularised the idea so much, that people came to accept the cereal as an important item on their breakfast table.

There are numerous examples where opportunities are created by presenting things in a different and, in an appealing way; or just, by educating people in different uses of a thing, apart from its common use. The more uses a thing has, the greater is the need for it e.g. water, electricity.

Some people may not realise, that opportunities may actually exit in many different forms. It only requires an inquisitive mind to perceive them. The best way to start hunting for an opportunity, is to look no further than your own doorstep. In short, look at your own surroundings, your own self, and ask yourself the following simple questions:

- What do I do?
- What do I like best?,
- What are my hobbies, my pastimes?
- What kind of people live around me?

In most cases, you may quickly see, a link between your answers to the above questions and an opportunity which could be exploited to bring you cash. An example could be your hobby. Suppose you like drawing and painting. Ask yourself:

"Can I use my hobby to earn me cash?"

The more you will think about it, the more positive your thoughts will become, so that, in the end, your brain will start putting forward some lucrative propositions to you—triggering off some positive action on your part, starting with the formulation of a plan like this:

"Yes, I can make money from my hobby. Well, let me see in how many ways."

And those ways could be:

- I could teach others to draw.
- I will write a small 'How to...' guide on the subject.
- I will present my paintings in an exhibition.
- I will do mass-copying of my paintings and sell them via mail order, etc.

Each of the above propositions promise an income—may be a lot of it. The example shows that an opportunity could be right in front of your eyes, provided you can see and use it.

To create wealth, therefore, a person must not only be prepared to recognise opportunities, he must, actually, hunt for them. To stretch the point a little further, he must create them.

TIME AND OPPORTUNITIES

Opportunities have a time span. They can appear and disappear over time, like the Klondike Gold Rush. They can make one rich, sometimes overnight, IF they are recognised and used in the proper time.

Time can also be regarded as double-edged sword. It can both destroy and create opportunities. A florist, for instance, can make money as long as his flowers are fresh. As soon as they start wilting with the passage of time, they lose value. On the other hand, certain things increase in value with the passage of time e.g. classic cars, famous oil paintings, property. But that may not always be the case. An economic recession, for example, can turn what looked like an opportunity of making a financial gain, into a sad financial loss. Thus time can be an enemy as well as a friend. It can be your best friend, if you remain alert to changes around you, so that you can go on discovering fresh opportunities, in many different forms—even during a recession!

The world has passed through many opportunity "phases" over the centuries and will continue to do so in many different ways. For example, America offered vast opportunities for the early settlers: there was abundance of land to be had. Many poor immigrants of yesterday are millionaires of today. Then later, Africa opened up for the wealth-seekers. Then again, very recently, The Middle East oil boom came on the scene, creating high demand for Western technology, mushrooming into high-income employment opportunities for thousands of people from all over the world.

As time changes, so do the opportunities. TIME IS MONEY. An aspiring money maker must respect it. It can make one rich or poor. And it goes hand in hand with the opportunities.

Assume a person wishes to purchase a certain property and has savings of 10,000. He wishes to buy a three-bedroom house which costs 100,000. He finds that he needs only 5% deposit to go ahead, but the building society will lend him only 55,000, the maximum according to his annual income. That means, he cannot purchase the property he desires.

A two-bed room house is available at 60,000. He knows, that property prices are increasing at the rate of 20% per annum. He also knows, that he can earn a maximum of 1,000, net interest per annum on the 10,000 he has if he kept it in a savings account. His regular earnings would, however, remain unchanged.

What should he do?

He can do one of the following things:

1. Save for a few years, and then buy the desired property (3-bedroom)
2. Buy a two bed-room house now; sell it later to buy a three-bedroom one at an opportune time.
3. Forget about buying at all.

The results of the alternatives are considered below:

	Two-bedroom	Three-bedroom
Price now :	60,000	100,000
Deposit Available :	10,000	10,000
Loan required :	50,000	90,000
Loan Available :	55,000	55,000
Price after a year*:	72,000	120,000
Loan Obtained :	50,000	N/A
Proceeds (if sold after one year)	22,000	N/A
Less repayments on loan (say @ 12%) :	6,000	N/A
Net Benefit :	16,000	N/A

* Price now plus 20% rise

Buying the three-bedroom house is out of question, in the present circumstances. It is clear, that he would be better off following alternative 2, i.e. buy the two-bedroom house NOW. This will make him 6,000 richer by the end of a year, i.e. 16,000 less the deposit of 10,000. Not buying at all would make him 'poor' by 6,000, ignoring interest received, and costs related to purchase and sale.

This very simple example illustrates the importance of time in relation to an opportunity. Time, therefore, is of an essence in getting rich. Imagine TIME as an express train, thundering away towards some future destinations; at each destination there is a hoard of treasure, waiting to be picked up by the passengers. One must 'hop' on the train at the earliest to get to those 'treasures.'

Time and opportunities, thus, go hand in hand. Grabbing an opportunity in the right time can make the difference between success and failure; between a poor man and a rich man.

Very often, a person who has missed an opportunity, will regret and say something like this:

"Wish I had thought of this before!"

"Wish I had bought that property earlier!"

"Wish I had listened to his advice!"

We all regret doing or not doing something at certain times. But as they say:

"It is never too late"; or

"Better late than never."

Mistakes of past should, in fact, become the stepping stones for tomorrow's success.

Often, people who have suffered a loss of some sort, losing a job, for example, have been noticed to bide away their time in unnecessary worrying. To make the matters worse, they start squandering away any savings they may have had on 'useless' things. Under the pretext of 'passing time', they may spend it on heavy drinking or other wasteful pleasures. Often they would start gambling—hoping to make big wins which may never happen.

Saving is a first step towards getting rich. It is a form of money-making, while spending money away recklessly, or wasting it, is just opposite of it, and could lead to hardship.

In fact, any cessation of regular income should start one's brain ticking. One should consider the 'free time' available when unemployed, as a 'lucky' break; it could gainfully be used in discovering various means of making cash, and not of losing it.

Respect TIME in relation to available opportunities. The TIME will then respect you by bringing you the riches you desire.

Meet The Lady Luck

Some people tend to believe, that luck plays a big role in bringing someone wealth. It could be true in a sense, but then, one has to see what luck, actually is, and to whom does it favour.

Luck is a mystery which no one really, ever, understood. However, what we call luck is, actually, a 'chance happening' and, may be of two kinds:

One is as a result of a pure chance, something which one could not have visualised beforehand. The other is something which, one expects to happen, but with a varying degree of certainty.

For instance, imagine you find a large, raw diamond, worth thousands of pounds in the bush, while out on say, an African safari. This you would call luck—something which occurred as a result of a pure chance. You were not out there looking for diamonds, but just on a pleasure trip. You could not have foreseen finding of the diamond.

On the other hand, if you had gone into the jungle looking for diamonds, and found one, then it was something you were looking forward to, something you were expecting to happen, although the certainty of its happening would have varied from 0% to 100%.

The above example reveals the two-fold nature of luck—the luck which is seeking you, and, the luck which you are seeking. The former is something which could happen, but cannot be foreseen; the latter is something you want to make it happen, and for which, you are deliberately taking a chance by doing something, to see it happen. Here we are concerned with the second type of luck—a chance you are deliberately taking. And that is what really counts in the business world, and in the money-making game.

For example, if you leave your full-time employment, and go into business, then you are taking a chance to create your own luck, that is, expecting to make lots of money. Whether you will succeed in making 'lots of money', is something, you cannot really predict, but you are optimistic, that you will make good money. This is where you are purposely seeking to influence your luck, by taking a chance, or as we usually call it, a risk. If you succeeded in your business venture, then you would call yourself 'lucky.'

Thus, those who take a chance and ACT, are actually going after luck, and usually, succeed in finding it, because both their physical and mental capabilities are working towards a single purpose. On the contrary, those who just depend on a chance happening of something, without any action on their part, are, in fact, courting 'bad luck', because they let opportunities pass them; their whole concentration remains pinned on a single, freak happening which they cannot influence, e. g. a big win at the football pools or a lottery of some kind. Such luck-seekers are like the lonely gold prospector who spends all his life looking for "the shiny metal", but never finds it.

The Lady Luck is full of glamour and charms, but she is also very elusive. People who depend on her coming to them automatically, may never even see her face. She usually favours and smiles over those who go after her.

There is a story about a man who started believing in fate or luck only, when he heard a priest saying:

"God has undertaken to provide man with his bread. As long as he is going to live, God will feed him somehow."

The man thought: "Since God will provide me with food, then why should I toil for it so much."

And so, he sat down in a busy street, hoping his food will, somehow, come to him. Three days passed. No one gave him even a morsel of bread. Hunger made him weak and miserable. A wise old man, noticing his plight, stopped by, and said:

"You have all your limbs intact. Why don't you work for living?"

The 'beggar' recounted to him what the priest had said. The old man smiled and said:

"Don't be like a fox that feeds on bread crumbs of others. Be like a lion who hunts and kills, not only to feed itself, but some other creatures as well. "

CONSTRAINTS TO FINANCIAL FREEDOM

For most people, a paid employment is the only obvious choice for making a living. Finding a worth while job, and keeping it, is their main goal. And what happens then? Their whole physical and mental efforts are concentrated towards that single source of income. The '9 to 5' routine becomes a way of life for them. They become so glued to a set pattern of living, that they seldom bother to look around, to notice other ways of making a living— through self-employment, for example. Very few actually do.

A person who holds some academic or professional qualifications, usually, feels secure in a job, or believes, that if he loses one, he can always get another. He may be right, but there is always a degree of risk in working for others. One could be sacked or made redundant at any time. And to lose a job, at a time when one most needs it, is devastating.

There are people who may continue working for others, but a time comes when they may feel fed up of the 'daily grind', especially, if their earnings were not so good. Many would, at times, grumble and say:

"Wish I was rich!"

The words may be uttered in sheer desperation, but then, do they ever turn around, and think seriously of changing their lives when the going is good; of going into self-employment? Very few people really do. Most would give it a passing thought only and carry on as usual. But often, some would come out with their real feelings when asked. They would say something like the following:

"I do not have enough capital."

"I do not really know what I can do. "

"I don't think I can be a businessman."

Such statements seem to reflect narrow thinking, and is a sort of self-denial. It will only act as a constraint to their ever succeeding in life; of taking a major step forward towards financial independence. It will keep holding them back. People in this category may never make it 'big' unless it was through 'sheer luck'. Their life is like a one-way street.

On the other hand, there are some who wish to go for self-employment, but the fear of putting at risk any savings they have had, deters them from doing so. Hence, they prefer to stick to the well-trodden path—the '9 to 5' routine—to which they, virtually, have become slaves. They are 'busy' earning their money. But actually speaking, they are not earning the way they should be earning, i. e. through self-employment—the only way to big income and wealth. Someone has rightly said about people who toil for a fixed wage, that they are "too busy earning than to earn anything."

People who seriously want financial freedom, do not prefer to work for others, at least, not for ever. They are always on the lookout for self-employment opportunities they can grab. Many would have a go at anything which can bring them extra cash. Some may continue to work for others, but also have a second source of income of some sort. This extra income enables them to save more, and acts as an assurance against any uncertain future hardship they may have to contend with. Losing a job, for example.

There is yet another category of people. They are those who work for others, but only to bide their time, and to save as much as they can. Their main aim is to go into business at some opportune time. They always think ahead, planning and keeping their future into focus. They treat their current jobs as a training ground for acquiring experience which they would use to their advantage later. They accumulate business ideas and keep themselves informed of opportunities, wherever they may exist. When the time is right, they would leave their jobs and go straight into business. They never, however, rush into things, but advance sure and steady. Most get rich in a very short time.

Many immigrants to advanced countries like U. S. A. and the U.K., fall in this category. Most of them may not even be very highly educated or skilled, but the success in business enables them to buy the skills they may need to run their businesses. They start as employees and end up as bosses.

THE JOB MARKET SCENARIO

The business world has gone through rapid changes over the last few years. Industrialised countries are now facing competition from many new sources, especially The Far East, where the labour cost is relatively lower. The rising cost of production and shrinking shares in the world markets has forced businesses to improve their organisational styles and manufacturing methods.

Automation has thus assailed our offices and factories. The increasing use of computers and the gradual proliferation of robots in many sectors of the industrial world, are casting dark clouds over the demand for human labour, especially, where repetitive, monotonous activities are involved.

Today's industrial environment thus, presents a completely different job scenario from the one which existed a few years ago. New skills are being sought by employers, especially, those in the high-tech fields. The management of large organisations is getting more and more complex and sophisticated. The pace of international trade is increasing owing to improvements in communications. There is increasing mobility of labour as the air travel becomes easier and cheaper. All this has created demand for very high and specialised skills generally.

Looking at present, it appears, that future orientation of businesses is towards high quality at minimum cost. This means increasing use of computers and industrial robots to accomplish tasks previously performed by humans. All this heralds great changes in management styles and production methods which could affect the demand for the common worker possessing rudimentary skills only.

On the other hand, the highly skilled person will be much in demand and would command high earnings. However, the uncertainty of losing a job will always be there. When the industry faces a slump, not only the unskilled and the semi-skilled suffer, the highly skilled may also have to bear the brunt of it.

The present trend, therefore, indicates the demise of many employment opportunities in the future, especially, where heavy physical effort is required, since more and more mechanical and electronic methods will take over. The highly specialised methods would require people with highly specialised skills. The acquisition of those skills may get more and more expensive, and, may require longer periods of studies, which again, people with high incomes only, would manage to give to their children.

This brings us to the point we are trying to make. And that is, that the only way open to an ordinary person for maintaining a good standard of living in the future, would be through having a business of his own. It wouldn't matter whatever happens to the future of jobs then.

HELP FOR THE BUSINESS MINDED

A person can create wealth anytime if he happens to be at the RIGHT PLACE at the RIGHT TIME. A real money maker doesn't wait for things to happen. He makes them happen. An upsurge in U.K.'s economy in the late eighties, for example, created an environment in which, anyone who went for self-employment, may have greatly benefited provided, of course, if he had used the opportunities available properly.

The demand for consumer goods is ever on the increase. This has resulted in increased public spending, despite high cost of borrowed money. The gradual lowering of rate of taxation for both the individuals and the businesses, has given a boost to the demand for goods and services, which in turn, has resulted in increased business activity. A favourable environment, therefore, has been created for seriously business-minded people—people who prefer self-employment against a paid employment, i. e. working for someone.

Most governments have schemes designed to help individuals set up their own business. In U.K. an Enterprise Allowance, given to individuals in their first year of business, is an example of the kind of help available. Information, advice and help can be obtained from many sources. It is up to the aspiring money-maker to make use of the facilities available in his own country.

Addresses of some U.K. organisations which could be of use to an individual living in the U.K., are included in Appendix IV.

But before one could start any business, one needs funds. Over the last decade, there has been significant changes in the lending habits of many financial institutions in the U.K. In the past, for example, usually building society funds were available to individuals wishing to buy properties.

18

Today most financial institutions, like banks and insurance companies, have also entered the mortgage market. And with the formation of the European Community, the credit market is widening still further. The result is that one has an easy access to funds today than some years ago. The credit squeeze of a few years back, seems to be the thing of the past. For the ordinary wealth-seeker, there couldn't be a better time to excel. The TIME to make big money could be here and now.

You only need to come up with some brilliant business idea to get hold of the funds available. And a true wealth creator, we must remember, creates his wealth by using less of his own money and more of others'—by borrowing of course.

WATCH WHERE YOU ARE GOING

Once you have set your eyes on a chosen idea, you must plan to put it into action. Planning is a must, whether it is for a wedding, or just for going on a holiday. And planning for business is no exception. Rushing into things, without full preparation often leads to confusion, frustration, disappointment, or even failure.

Planning for self-employment can commence with conception of some money-making idea, and, collection of facts about it. The details in the plan would vary according to the nature of work, or the type of business you would wish to go for.

Let us suppose you wish to purchase a shop of some kind. This would involve stating your requirements in relation to the nature of business you wish to acquire, it's location and other essential facts about it. It would also involve taking stock of resources available to you.

One of the essential feature of your plan would be a financial evaluation of a business you may intend to purchase. It could, for example, be in the form of a questionnaire. A specimen form is included in Appendix I.

Planning ensures maintenance of proper sequence in accomplishing various stages in the plan, with minimum wastage of human effort, time and money. Various specialised planning techniques are used by today's businesses. A typical technique is known as Critical Path Analysis, where an activity chart is used to plan the completion of given operation or a project. The chart highlights the critical activities on which the completion time, and the cost, of the whole project would depend.

For example, a plan for buying a shop may involve activities as under:

Activities Time	Taken (days)
Obtain details of shops on sale	10
Study the details	5
Make a short list of suitable ones	4
Evaluate them	6
Select the best one	2
Negotiate the purchase of it	3

And so on.

Of course, any decision to purchase a business would involve seeking of professional advice from say, an accountant, who would be fully aware of various business planning and evaluating techniques.

Planning should be meticulous. It should be complete and comprehensive, and showing clear directions towards achievement of your goal. The main components of you plan would require you to state:

(a) Your objective clearly and concisely.

(b) The resources required to achieve the plan.

(c) The resources you have at your disposal.

(d) Any money you need to borrow.

(e) The method you would employ to succeed in your plan.

(f) The expected income you would derive from the success of your plan.

Let us assume you, that you intend to make money as a part-time driving instructor, operating from home. You may, for instance, draw up a simple plan as follows:

OBJECTIVE:

To start a part-time driving school business, operating from home. I will still keep my present job until I need it.

RESOURCES REQUIRED

- Driving instructor's licence (ADI). A two-week intensive course would cost, say	400
- A small second-hand car, to start with. Cost:	4000
- A name, sign board, etc.,	100

RESOURCES AVAILABLE

- Savings to date:	2000
- Net savings per week from full time job:	100

MONEY NEED TO BORROW

Funds required:

- Course fee		400
- Motor car		4000
- Name, sign board, fixtures, etc.		100
- Working capital		100
	Total	4600
Funds Available:		2100
Funds need to borrow:		2500

METHOD OF OPERATION

- I will teach driving in the evenings and over the weekends.
- I will attract clients by advertising in local papers, and/or by distributing leaflets. I also have many personal contacts, friends and relations who can help spread the news of my services.

- I will charge 10 an hour to start with, and increase to 12 when I am fully established.

EXPECTED INCOME

- 3 Hours per day (Mon-Fri) @ 10 per hour: 3 x 5 x10=150
- 10 hours over the week end: 10 x 10=   100
                                                                                          _____

- Gross weekly income =   250
- Less Costs: (Fuel + ins + maint+ depr +int)=   150
                                                                                          _____

- Net Weekly income (25 hours)=   100
                                                                                          _____

- Annual Income before tax: 100x 48 weeks (say)=   4800
                                                                                          _____

The above is an illustration of a simple business plan. The figures could, of course, be projected to include more operating hours by, say employing your wife or hiring outside drivers as you expand. Having a business plan in front of you would enable you to know exactly where you stand, where you are going, and the limit you can expand to; and the income you would generate. The plan would also form a basis for convincing your bank manager to lend the extra funds you may need.

Whatever your aims and ambitions about making big money, plan for it. Planning acts as a device for spurring you on towards your goal. It will not only force your attention on the problems you could encounter in achieving it, it would also guide you towards situations you could use to your best advantage as you go along.

PATHWAYS TO WEALTH CREATION

Most ordinary people wish to be rich, but may not know where or how to make a start. As mentioned earlier, a certain kind of 'luck' has to be sought by a person himself. He has to create his own favourable circumstances , in order to gain the financial freedom he desires.

In the following pages, you will read about some of the proven ways to achieve that. Call them what you will—a successful money maker's 'Golden Tips', or a wealth-seeker's 'Magic Keys'. But, we are positive, they should lead you to that chance happening which you may be earnestly seeking. Just follow the 'pathways' and experience the glamour and thrill of making BIG MONEY.

Find That 'Golden' Person

If you are not already in business, then meet people who are. This will 'condition' your mind to think like them. However, meeting the right kind of 'golden' person is not always easy. A good idea is to start with someone you already know, as he will be more willing to guide and help. For example, he may propose a course of action for you to follow, or perhaps, put you in touch with someone who 'knows'.

Remember that the driving force behind the business world are people—people who have the know-how, and, can give you the impetus to succeed in your objective. Just by watching an expert in action, could inspire you to go ahead and do what you wanted to do, but were always afraid to.

Some people may not disclose their business secrets, even to their closest friends, let alone to a stranger. But if you are tactful, you can glean lot of useful information through say, a friendly chat. Sometimes you may just 'stumble over' some very useful piece of information just by listening carefully to people chatting with each other. What you need, is an alert mind, to observe what is going on around you; a sort of antenna to feel the business waves flowing past you.

When you are talking to a business person, try finding out certain facts that can give you some insight into his methods, through which he succeeded in achieving his goal. For example, try discovering:
- How did he break into business?
- What products or services is he dealing in?
- Where does he buy them from, and at what price?
- How and where does he sell them?
- Are his goods or services in short supply?
- Are they in good demand?
- What is his turnover?
- How much profit does he make?
- How did he finance his business?
- How much capital is required for that kind of business?

Even an ordinary person, who sells fancy balloons in a busy high street, is in business, and may have, some useful tips up his sleeve.

No one person has been given complete knowledge of everything in this world, but each individual has, at least, some share of the total knowledge that exits. Meeting all sorts of people doesn't hurt, since the 'golden' person holding the key to your financial success, could be any one of them. He may not, necessarily, be a business person, but still have some useful hints or ideas which could put you on the road to riches.

Visit New Places

Some people would live in a place for years without ever visiting another town, let alone another country. As an aspiring wealth-seeker, it could be a good idea to get around.

One would argue, that a person need not necessarily visit a new place to look for opportunities, since today's mass media can give him enough information about what is happening elsewhere. True, but not the kind of 'inside' information which a real wealth-seeker would prefer to have.

The whole idea of visiting a place is to discover, at first hand, the opportunities that exist and about which the media may not offer full coverage. Visiting a place in person means creating your own 'lucky' circumstances, watching the business in action, and meeting different people among whom you may find your 'golden' person i. e. someone who could give you the right ideas, to enable you to alter the course of your life.

Only by visiting a place personally, can one get a real close-up of the opportunities lurking behind the scenes, and which, only a truly business-minded person can perceive. Seeing is believing. Watching something at close range can trigger off the thinking process which generates ideas. What we actually see with our own eyes, and hear with our own ears, appears more credible than what others tell us about.

It does not imply that one should embark on a world tour to seek opportunities. No ordinary person can afford that, nor is it necessary. However, it helps to visit a place about which you might have heard some good rumours. For example, people seek jobs in the Gulf because they hear that one could earn a good, tax-free income there.

An ordinary person may visit a place for a holiday, i. e. for pleasure. An opportunity-seeker may do it for both business and pleasure. The idea is to explore an environment in full and to see what it can best offer. Mixing with the 'crowd' gives you the real feel of the place.

An unemployed car mechanic, during a holiday in an African country, discovered that there was an acute shortage of cars and all types of consumer goods in the country, and things cost almost four times higher than in his own country. He clinched a deal with a native businessman to supply him second-hand cars, TVs and videos. Despite foreign exchange restrictions in the native's country, he managed to get paid somehow. Within a few years, he had enough capital to establish a large full-time exporting business of his own.

There are lot of such examples where people have changed their 'luck' by visiting a new place. An ordinary clerk, during a visit to a Gulf state, noticed that there was a big demand for some essential video and television parts in the country. And a sole dealer was charging exorbitant prices to local repair shops. Having some knowledge of the parts, he took orders from a number of repair shops, agreeing to supply them the parts on very preferential terms. Twice a year, he travelled to a Far Eastern country, purchased the parts and returned within a week to dispose them off for hard cash and a handsome profit. Within a couple of years, he had made enough money to go into a business partnership with a rich national there.

Perhaps, that is what one would call: "Being at the right PLACE at the right TIME !"

Identify a Need

You cannot make money if you don't have anything to sell. You cannot sell anything unless people need what you want to sell, and, are willing to part with their money in exchange for it. As a potential money maker you must, therefore, find out what people really want, at a particular time, and at a particular place. Look around, and you will notice, that everywhere, all the time, some sort of need is being satisfied for which people are paying. It could be a product, or simply, a service of some sort.

Needs may differ from people to people, but there are always some needs which are common to all people: food, clothing, shelter, transport. All these are everyday needs and, are catered for, by someone or the other. One might say: "Well there is someone satisfying that need, so what chance do I have?"

This is negative thinking, and reflects ignorance of the whole money-making concept. If you walk down any busy street in your town, you will observe, that there are always some shops which supply similar products or services. They all attract custom, otherwise they wouldn't be there. The secret is in the individuality of each customer's needs, and the style of service offered by each shop. Each business has its own unique personality, including the staff who serve the customers. There may be, for instance, variations in the quality, models, colour, or size of the products they sell; maybe it is the way the goods are displayed or priced which differs; or perhaps, it is simply, a different approach to the customer.

The whole money-making process, in fact, revolves around the basic needs mentioned above. From these basic needs all other human wants or sub-needs arise. For example, food. One person may prefer to have a meal in a posh hotel; another one enjoys it having in a busy restaurant; yet another person may go for a quick snack from a take-away type. They all have a common need—food, but each wants to satisfy it differently. All eating places can satisfy the need for food, but each is different in terms of quality, price or just the look of it.

A firm makes simple serving trays, but in a variety of shapes, sizes and colours. A tray is a tray, but the variety appeals to the public, and thus, generates income for the firm.

In studying a need, consideration must be given to the various factors, especially, the following:

- The timing of providing a service or a product.
- The place where it is going to be provided.
- The people it is going to be provided to, i.e. their habits, customs, interests, lifestyles, etc.

The above points are very important. Ignoring them would show lack of business intuition, which means no business, and, no money.

For example:

- You will sell more ice-cream in summer than in winter—a seasonal need.
- No Arab country would buy your meat products, unless the animal, from which the meat came, was slaughtered in an Islamic way—a need conforming to religion.

It all boils down to the fact, that not only must you identify a need, you must also identify the various forms in which it has to be satisfied. Only then can you make a fortune from your business ventures.

Increase Your Knowledge

Knowledge is a great power. It is through the miracles of knowledge that man has built great things: aeroplanes, skyscrapers, computers, space rockets—just to name a few. The fruits of knowledge are in such abundance, that one cannot count them. Knowledge, actually, is the life-blood of man's achievements. We may give different names to ' Knowledge', but it is the same knowledge which we have divided and classified into different categories or under different scientific names: physics, chemistry, biology, archaeology, etc.

Knowledge seems to have no end. What knowledge we have acquired up till now, could only be a tiny drop of the vast ocean which exists in the whole universe. There are certain things which had existed all the time, but man discovered them through the ages; for example, electricity.

There could be lot of other things which may exist, but man has yet to discover; scores of mysteries to unearth. Any discovery which will contribute towards satisfying various needs of man, is sure to generate wealth. Discovery of oil and gas are giant examples.

Just imagine, for example, someone discovering a metal which defies the forces of gravity. It would be a blockbuster. It would open the gates of wealth for its discoverer, and also, for many of his fellow beings. It would enable man to fly without the aid of noisy aeroplanes!

Knowledge, however, can take various forms. For example, if we saw someone flying without the aid of any physical means, we might call him a magician or a sorcerer. Whether it is a sorcery or magic, or hypnotism, it is still a science, although of a different kind, and about which, a common man may not have much knowledge. An aspiring money maker would, of course, acquire knowledge which will enable him to succeed in business, not perform magical tricks, though money-making itself, has its own magical charm about it.

When we talk about knowledge, we also talk about information. The latter builds up knowledge. A well-informed person has an edge over his fellow beings and stands to gain most of the time.

Knowledge could be acquired formally or informally. The former knowledge is acquired when one, purposely undertakes a course of study. An informal knowledge comes automatically from exposure to the world around us, through pieces of information obtained from various sources.

If you wish to succeed in reaching the threshold of financial freedom, then you must acquire knowledge, especially, of the business world, and the related opportunities. Keep yourself informed of what is happening around you. There are many ways of doing that. Some are as follows:

- *Do a lot of reading.*

Read anything, especially: newspapers, specialised magazines and journals, newsletters, etc. Even a casual browse through a magazine or a newspaper at a newsagent, could give you a vital piece of information and 'set you on'. It could be just a small advertisement you happen to see.

- *Watch business programmes on television.*
- *Listen to business talk on the radio.*
- *Talk to people in business, or anyone who could give you important piece of information.*

Many magazines and newspapers, both national and international, could be recommended for regular reading. A short list of some of the relevant ones available in the U.K. are presented below:

Auto Trader
Car Auction Magazine
Dalton's Weekly
Exchange and Mart
Money
Overseas Job Express
Property International
Property Mail
The Economist magazine
The Dealer
The Financial Times, and other serious newspapers.
The Mortgage Magazine
Trader
What Investment?

The above list is not intended to be exhaustive. There are scores of other publications which cater for specialised interest, and which you may like to read occasionally, to supplement your knowledge about a particular subject. Many individual organisations also publish newsletters or magazines, designed to inform subscribing members of latest money making ideas. Information on these are often advertised in the business section of the daily press.

Many publications now have their web page on the internet and can be read online; not only that, you can download information and articles from their sites for later use. In fact, the internet is becoming a vast ocean of knowledge. A click of a button on your PC keyboard can bring, virtually, any information you need within seconds on to your computer screen, thus saving you a lot of time and cost.

Thus, armed with Knowledge, you cannot go wrong in whatever you are planning to do. The fact is that KNOWLEDGE will snowball you towards success.

Acquire Business Power Through a Skill

As stated earlier, you cannot make money unless you have something to sell—a product or service which people need. To sell the product or service, you need the skill to make the product or render the service. Skill and knowledge go hand in hand. They give you a start, and enable you to win at the money-making game.

If you haven't had a chance to acquire any formal qualifications, don't worry. There are certain skills which you can acquire over a very short period. And people with ordinary skills, at times, make more money than a person does after years of college education. The reason is, that with certain skills, you can become self-employed, enabling you to earn a big, variable income, unlike the person in a paid employment, earning a limited pay only.

Remember, technology is changing fast. You must keep pace with it to be in the forefront of good income-earners. Any new skill you acquire, may not only win you a good job, it would enable you to earn a spare-time income as well. It could lead you to a thriving business of your own one day.

Some people would hate the idea of going back to school, especially after they have passed certain age and were working full time. However, there are many types of skills which could be acquired in a short period of time—a couple of weeks to six months, yet give you a start towards making some cash for yourself. Consider, for example, short courses like: car repairs, TV/Video repairs, hairdressing, driving instruction, computer operator, etc. Your primary aim is to increase your immediate earnings, especially, if you are really hard up.

With advancement in technology, there are more opportunities now to earn large sums of money than ever before, especially, from skills related to Information Technology. In fact, some short-term IT courses—lasting from a week or two—can enable any ordinary person, to earn more money than someone who has spent a few years to acquire an academic degree. After acquiring IT skills, some people go into business of their own e.g. building computers or providing Consulting services to their local industry.

There is no better field than IT for anyone who has had no chance of acquiring higher education which can be expensive and needs long period of continuous, full time study. With IT, one can go on enhancing one's skills by attending short-term courses, as more and more systems come on to the market. Moreover, IT speaks a common language; it is not ruled by each country's special institutional regulation, like Accountancy, for example, where tax laws differ in each country. With IT, the whole world of opportunities is open to one.

Many private institutions conduct continuous short-term courses on various subjects on an intensive basis. One could, for example, easily use one's leave period to attend some of the courses if one is employed full time.

It may sometimes be observed, that while a person with higher managerial skills may join the dole queue if he happened to lose his job, the one with some basic skills would continue to earn his living, by say, offering some common service from home e.g. body massage, TV repairs, etc. The idea is to keep the cash flowing in.

In most advance countries, the government also takes active role in training people. In U.K., for example, The Department of Employment has established many special schemes to train people in various skills, especially, those who have been unemployed for six months or more. The training is designed to enhance a person's existing skills, or even, help him to acquire new skills, in order to get him back to work. A person is free to choose a skill in which he wishes to be trained. There is also a scheme, as mentioned earlier, which is designed to train people in setting up a business of their own, with some cash help from the government. Such schemes are very beneficial, and have helped many unemployed people in returning to worthwhile jobs, or in becoming self-employed. Do make use of facilities available in your own country, and start building a sound, financial future for yourself.

Invent and Grow Rich

Could you invent something which could appeal to the public at large? Nothing could be a better money-spinner than that. Look at all those gadgets: television, vacuum cleaners, toasters, washing machines, motor cars, computers—to name a few. All these have revolutionised the concept of wealth creation.

Remember, anything which satisfies some basic need, reduces human effort, gives comfort, pleasure, and speeds up the finishing of tasks, is sure to be a winner.

You would say: "How can I possibly invent anything? I am not a scientist!" Well, you don't have to be. A simple bright idea, which may suddenly crop up in your mind, can result in an invention by someone else, bringing both of you fame and fortune.

Suppose you said to a friend one day:

"I wish there was a machine which could shave my beard automatically every morning."

Imagine your friend was an engineer who was looking for ways to make big money. The idea might strike him as a 'golden one'. His brain might start ticking and receiving 'messages' or images of "the gadget that will shave a beard automatically."

Suppose he goes ahead and succeeds in making such a machine. Wouldn't it sell like hot cakes? It surely would, because most men would love to buy it.

All the gadgets we are using today are the brainchild of some THINKING mind. All satisfy human needs and, therefore, create wealth for their manufacturers.

An invention, more often, starts with a need or a necessity, and conceived through an IDEA. An idea is like a hidden treasure. Many people would pay large sums of money just to buy an idea.

An idea is a 'golden' one if it appeals to masses. Any idea or invention which will satisfy the needs of the public at large, is sure to burst the gates of riches for its originator, and many others as well. Things like a toilet roll, an ice cream on a cone or the changing traffic signals, are all results of someone's bright suggestion—someone who wasn't a scientist. They are mass-produced items, used world-wide, and so generate wealth for their manufacturers.

Very often, we may get some 'golden' idea in our brain, but it may also disappear quickly. The reason is that we are often too busy to give it a further thought, or maybe, we reckoned it wasn't of direct benefit to us at the time. Human thoughts are very fluid and susceptible to quick changes. Many good ideas thus fade away as soon as they appear. As a potential money-maker you cannot afford to do that. Make a note of any idea you get, especially, if it relates to man's needs. However trivial it may seem at the time, it could turn out to be a real money-spinner in the light of some new developments in the future. You never know.

In the modern, competitive business environment, it is a do or die situation for most businesses. Innovation is the keynote for business success today. Hence, many companies, especially, in the U.S.A., are always on the lookout for new ideas or inventions which will enable them to create wealth, or even, to survive. And they pay large sums of money for them.

Most large companies today, have their own specialised team of experts whose job is to churn out fresh ideas, i. e. create new products or services or, just improve the existing ones. Members of such a team make deliberate attempts at generating ideas. During, what is called, a 'brainstorming' session, members put forward suggestions, which are recorded, however simple they may seem. Later, their ideas are sifted, analysed and studied in detail. Best ones are then selected and tried. This results in a completely new or improved product which generates further wealth for the owners of the company.

As stated earlier, human thoughts have no bounds. They can reach the furthest boundaries of the universe, like the rays of sunlight reaching the earth over million of miles.

A bright idea can spring up at any time in our brain, especially, when we may be thinking of some problem, or engaged in doing something. A young American boy often brushed his dog to get rid of lice stuck in the animal's fur. The dog also wore a special, medicated belt around its neck to repel the lice, but it wasn't very effective.

One day the lad got an idea. He passed a hot domestic iron over the dog's fur to get rid of the pest. To his surprise, the lice fell down dead, killed by the heat from the iron. This triggered off new thoughts in his brain. He went along and produced a brush having strands made from steel wire which could be electrically heated. He brushed the dog with it. That really did the trick: the brush picked the lice neatly out of the fur. It was the perfect and unique solution to the problem.

The lad quickly registered his invention. A company offered him a few million dollars for the rights to manufacture and market the brush. The boy was amazed to learn the value of his invention. As it goes, the boy made a counter offer to the company. The latter did not accept it, so the lad started his own firm to manufacture the brush. And it goes without saying, that he became a confirmed millionaire, almost overnight—just from a simple idea which arose in his mind.

Work Abroad

Working in another country offers great attraction to many people for various reasons. Some just seek adventure; for some it is like having a slow holiday, especially, when a place has some special features. Others are attracted by the high salaries offered by foreign employers, especially, if they are free of taxes, and include special perks like free housing, transport and medical.

Some people would go anywhere to earn big money. The harsh climatic conditions like the 'below-zero' temperature of Alaska, or the sweltering heat of the Gulf, do not deter them from venturing out to foreign lands. They are even prepared to suffer what is called a 'cultural shock'—the strange feeling of being in a different culture to one's own—in order to get rich.

It doesn't mean that all of us should venture out to work abroad, since not everyone's circumstances are alike. But if you get a chance to make good money overseas, by all means, take it. A few years abroad could change your lifestyle and swell your bank balance to a desirable figure. A visit to some new place, as discussed earlier, is sometimes very beneficial in many other ways. By actually staying in a place over a long period, you come to know more about it: its people, its good and bad points, and the opportunities it can offer.

Developing countries, for example, offer good opportunities for investing in businesses which can grow with the country. A pharmacist from a 'poor' country went to work in one of the Gulf countries. After a few years, he opened his own pharmacy. The business thrived with the oil boom. To day he owns medical centres in a number of Gulf countries—a self-made millionaire. The secret behind his success was his presence in a country which was experiencing an economic boom. By being there, he obtained first-hand knowledge of the place, and became exposed to the opportunities which were cropping up around him.

Many people have thus used their foreign jobs as a springboard for getting into big business later. Others return to their home countries, armed with full knowledge of the country they had lived in, which they use to their good advantage. For example, some start an import and export business with the countries they have been to. Others do business through agents, or even, enter into partnerships with foreign nationals.

There is no end to the ways people get rich, though some, in rather 'strange' ways. A rather interesting story is told about an expatriate who worked in a country where natives secretly sold precious stones, smuggled from the local mines, to foreigners at almost dirt value. The expatriate in question had collected a sack-full of them, and was looking for ways to smuggle them out of the country. He joined a local flying club. One day, while going on to one of his flying rounds, he took the gems aboard with him. Flying over a jungle near the border of a neighbouring country, he parachuted down, letting the plane crash into the forest below. The 'survivor' then crossed over the border into the 'friendly' country. From there, he boarded a plane bound for... Imagine the lengths some will people go to, to become rich! Nevertheless, it proves the point we are making.

Migrate

It is often said, that a CHANGE OF PLACE CAN CHANGE ONE'S LIFE AND BRING GOOD LUCK.

Some people would dismiss the assertion as 'nonsense'. But many, who have experienced improvement in their standard of living or general well-being by moving to another place agree, that it has an element of truth in it. Perhaps, there is some astrological explanation, we don't know. However, many people, who have migrated over the years to different countries, did not do it for fun. Many changed their lucks by exploiting the opportunities presented by foreign lands.

People have been migrating all the time for centuries. They are still doing it, especially, to the U. S. A., Canada, Australia, New Zealand and so on. It is human nature to seek romance, adventure and wealth. The world has become a small place today, as air travel has become more frequent and cheaper. More people travel nowadays than ever before, hence migration between countries has also become relatively simple.

Many people, from the East are thus migrating to the West to seek new opportunities. Others who posses some know-how, migrate to various developing countries in Asia and Africa to become rich by tapping the hidden resources there, or just to enjoy life in the tropics.

Migrating is a big step, especially, if one is going to settle in a country whose culture and climate is completely different to one's own. One should, therefore, consider the full implications of making the move.

Migration means complete uprooting and severing of ties with one's existing social and political environment and living away from close friends and relatives. It sometimes means leaving a whole, familiar world behind, and stepping into a completely different one, where one has to make a fresh start, and build a new future. The decision may be a difficult one, but taking the plunge could change one's life for the better. Sometimes it is advisable, to pay a visit to the country one intends to migrate to, before a permanent settlement there. The best way to know a country is to work there for a few years, after which one can decide for or against a permanent stay.

Some people often migrate to a country to live there for some years only. After they feel they had made enough money, they migrate back to their original country, to live comfortably for the rest of their lives, among old friends and relatives.

Living in a different country can widen one's general outlook and knowledge. Thus, many people who have spent some years in an advanced country, are often, seen to introduce new ideas to their home countries, and in the process, create tremendous money-making opportunities for themselves, and maybe others as well. The recent Americanisation of tastes in some European countries is an obvious example.

Visit Trade Shows / Exhibitions

Trade shows or exhibitions are held to inform the public as well as other organisations of products offered by different manufacturers. Under one roof, and in a short space of time, one could see a variety of different types and models. You also get an opportunity to discuss a product, which could include a demonstration or some further information on it. The whole atmosphere is business-like, and could 'charge' your thinking, giving you some new ideas of your own.

Many business-minded people use exhibitions and trade shows to obtain information about latest technology. The knowledge gives them an edge over their fellow businessmen, who may not be fully informed of new products or services in time to plan their business strategies.

If an exhibition can be used to display products of other people, it can be used to display yours. It is one of the popular and effective way of bringing a product in the eyes of the public, and especially, those who may show interest in buying them to further their own financial objectives. Exhibition gives a sort of prestige to your product and business. This is very important, especially, if you are trying to obtain an international recognition for it.

Sometimes you may not have enough funds to finance the production, distribution, or further development of a particular product. Since an exhibition or a trade show may be attended by all sorts of people, you may meet someone among them, who may have lot of funds at his disposal, and was on the lookout for new ideas. If your product showed a real potential, that person may offer to finance the production or development of it, or just offer you a large sum of money, for the rights to do it himself.

Information about the trade shows and exhibitions are often published in the press. Regular shows are, for example, held in U K at Olympia and Wembley Centre in London, and at the National Exhibition Centre in Birmingham, covering themes like Direct Marketing, Franchising, Information Technology, Inventions, etc. One can find many special offers and bargains at these shows, apart from gaining a first hand of knowledge various businesses, and new products and services. Thousands of people from different backgrounds and cultures attend these shows every year.

In fact, these shows are an excellent route to possible wealth creating ideas or opportunities. It could be a way of searching for that 'chance happening' which might bring you face to face with the Lady Luck.

Make Use of Fame and Fortune Relationship

Big fortunes can often be made by relating products or services to some famous place, thing, event or a person. A very good example is the 007 Bond image. Hundreds of spin-off products entered the market following the popularity of the Bond films.

Glamour, romance, heroism, sex, and adventure are very enchanting subjects; people always go with open arms for anything related to these. The young generation, especially, love to identify themselves with some famous heroes. They are readily attracted by anything reflecting the image of their idol, or reminds them of him of her.

Mark tee shirts, hankies, neckties, cuff-links or the like, with the picture of Elvis Presley or Marilyn Monroe and people will flock to buy them.

Articles can also be made to reflect attractions of certain famous places, e.g. Disneyland. In Africa, some places are often related to the country's wild life—a major tourist attraction there. For example, Kichiwa Tembo, a famous tourist spot in Kenya, which means 'Elephant Head' in the local language.

Some businesses may relate their products to famous people or celebrities e.g. kings, queens, artists, writers, poets or ancient heroes.

Others use certain anniversaries for timing the launch of new products e.g. birth of Shakespeare.

An important event, like the Christmas, and Independence Day Celebrations is a good opportunity for bringing out some innovating ideas involving toys, indoor games and other gifts which could sell like hot cakes. Some international sporting event like Soccer World Cup and Olympic Games also offer fantastic opportunities to cash in on some products related to these events e.g. badges, playing cards, coffee mugs, tea shirts, decorative balloons, etc. In fact, small items under $5.00 sell quickly. For example, if you just manage to sell a cheap item, say a metal badge costing a $1.00 with a $1.00 profit margin, to just 5000 people attending a football match, you can pocket $5000.00, clear.

Many people make huge amounts of money from such events by selling food items, like hot dogs, sandwiches. etc. There are thus, hundreds of ways of making big money by popularising your products or services by relating them to something important, or someone very close to the heart of the people, or an important event.

So why don't you try them. Get them right and then watch the tide of cash flow towards you.

Let People Know

You may have a very good product to offer, but people won't buy it unless they know what it is, and, where to buy it from. You have to let them know. And you do that through advertising.

The need to advertise may depend on the nature of your business, the products dealt in, and among other things, the length of time it has been in existence. If you are an ordinary shop-keeper in a busy high street, you may not consider the need for advertising, except for displaying your products attractively in the shop window.

Some businesses must advertise extensively to attract enough custom to survive. This happens when there is stiff competition from other similar businesses. You try to win sales by reaching as many potential customers as possible.

An advertising is a form of communication with the public at large. It enables you to reach masses at one go. Some businesses, due to their nature and management style, exist only by protracted advertising. Others employ different advertising techniques to sell their products. Mail Order firms, for example, advertise their goods through lavishly illustrated catalogues, given free to people interested in shopping through them.

Many ordinary people also use Mail Order selling techniques to generate big money. They advertise services or products in national newspapers, specialised trade journals or magazines, depending on the nature of the product they are trying to sell. Just one, single advertisement can, sometimes, attract orders worth thousands of pounds.

Imagine you want to sell a product on which you wish to make a profit of 1.00 per item. You advertise it in a national magazine read by say, a million people. If only 5% of the readers order your product, then you will make clean 50,000 cash—just from a single advertisement! That is the power of advertising in generating wealth.

The timing of an advertisement, and the choice of media, are important considerations for achieving success in selling your products. For example, advertising Christmas trees just after the Christmas won't pull many orders; advertising for women's lipstick in a magazine, mostly read by men, may not have the desired effect.

There are various advertising media which you can use for advertising your products: Weekly Advertisers, both national and local; trade journals, specialised magazines, national newspapers, radio and television. It all depends on how much you wish to spend and what impact you wish to have on the public.

To achieve the right impact, your advertisement must be professionally written. Writing an effective advertisement requires good knowledge, not only of the product being advertised, but also of the market it is intended for. A well-written advertisement can make the difference between success and failure of a business venture.

Quite a few books are available on the subject, giving useful hints on writing effective advertisements. However, if you are really going into big business, then leave the promotion and advertising of your products in the hands of experts, i. e. advertising agencies.

Advertising, in fact, has become the keyword for successful marketing of a company's products in the modern world. Some big organisations spend millions every year just to keep their products in the eyes of the public.

You don't have to own a big business to make a fortune. Find an item which people love to buy. It must be something new, in short supply, and one which satisfies a basic need. Sell it through advertising. A single entry in a popular newspaper or magazine could swamp you with orders. It could make you rich sooner than you could imagine.

Use the Power of Pool

Some people look at opportunities, but often let them pass, because they do not have enough funds to exploit them. As said earlier, time is of an essence in making money. Certain opportunities never repeat themselves.

By pooling resources, opportunities can be availed in the proper time. Resources are limited and scattered, but by combining them, one can create a larger resource which will help generate wealth. Large-scale production of goods by industries today would not have been possible without pooling of resources—funds contributed by large number of people, the shareholders.

The resources to be pooled together may not be just money; it could be anything which contributes towards attainment of a financial gain. For instance, a person may possess a particular skill or technical know-how, but no money to go into business. Another person may not possess any special skill, but could have access to large funds. By combining the two resources—the skill of one and the funds of the other—both stand to gain. Many big businesses of today came into existence that way.

A rather over-simplified example of benefits, derived from pooling of resources, would be where a number of people form a syndicate to bet on football pools. Each person contributes a small amount, but has a greater chance of a win, than if each had bet on his own, since the total amount staked is large.

Pooling of resources, not only increases the possibility of increased gains, it also speeds up the process of their realisation.

Unity Is Power, and, Many Hands Make Light Work—as we all know.

MONEY MAKERS IN ACTION— THE CASE BOOK

It is always interesting to know how other people get rich. Below we present a selection of real-life case studies, of ordinary people, who achieved financial independence through side business or full time self-employment, some starting from scratch. The names, however, have been changed to protect their identities. The cases, in fact, reflect the 'pathways' discussed earlier. Not only that, they also contain a wealth of information, which an aspiring money-maker, would find extremely useful in his search for big money. It is important to remember, that the cases selected, portray a cross-section of various business actions, situations, timing and environment rather than being just interesting stories. They are meant to show, that it is never impossible, for any ordinary man or woman, to earn money in many different ways, if only to meet his or her immediate financial commitments, instead of losing hope. And for the more ambitious, sky is the limit as you will discover.

Creating wealth through self-employment, rather than working for someone for a fixed pay, has all the ingredients of an exciting adventure itself, the thrills of which can only be felt by those who are prepared to, and have the guts to go through it. Like any adventure, it involves action, communication, travel, showing both physical and brain power pitted against many odds, presented by changing situations. In the business 'jungle' there are not only pitfalls and shaky bridges to scale, but also the joyful suspense, triumph of beating the odds and the pleasure of finding the 'treasure' in the end.

No wonder some millionaire aptly said, that there is more thrill in getting rich than actually being rich.

Now Please read on to discover how it all happens.

Case Number 1

"Some weeks I make more money than what my husband does…"

Sarah, a middle-aged housewife was always short of money. Her husband was an ordinary labourer whose wage was not enough to give them, and their three young children a comfortable life. The family was always in debt, until Sarah changed it all. Here is her story:

"I could never afford anything expensive," she said. "I often visited market stalls or swap meets for bargain buys. While there, I watched the market traders with interest, and would ask myself: 'Would they be making enough to justify their spending whole day at the stalls.' I ventured to ask one of the traders, who said: 'I sell all types of watches, especially, ones which everyone can afford. I make about 300 a week on average, sometimes half that amount on weekend alone.'

"It seemed incredible to me. I did further research. As the days passed, my brain was swamped with ideas. I felt almost dizzy with the thrill of making some cash, because I knew what I was going to do. I was going to hire a stall myself." And so she did.

She confides: " I sell children wear, mostly seconds or end of line items. I take a trip up North once a fortnight to buy them from the factories there. I get them cheap and sell them cheap. Most are branded wear which sell in the big stores at double the price I charge. Some items may be a little out of fashion, but they always sell fast. Most ordinary people are not rich and feel they are getting a bargain. On some days I make more money than what my husband earns in a month.

"After getting into this business, I have met people who are making large amounts of money. Many do not have any formal skills. The secret is in selling your stuff fast. And that, you can only do if, you sell it cheap.

But that is only possible if most people need what you want to sell and you can get it cheap and readily from somewhere.

"Many traders buy slightly damaged or liquidated stock at a fraction of what it would normally cost, and make a fortune out if it. Markets are held in most towns nowadays. Some people even take a weekend trip to the Continent to sell in the markets there, and return with pockets bulging with cash.

"Some big markets are visited by large number of shoppers, say three thousand people on a single weekend. Imagine you are selling something which is new and most people would need it. Say it cost you one dollar a piece, and you just wish to make one dollar profit on it. If only ten percent of the people buy it, you would make three hundred dollars in just one day. Imagine fifty percent of the shoppers buying it. You will be laughing all the way home with fifteen hundred dollars in your pocket!"

Commentary

This is a very simple case, but it shows, especially, to those brooding jobless or out of pocket, that it so simple to make money if one wishes to, without any special skills and, without having to toil a whole week or a month for it.

Case Number 2

"Discover this golden combination in your life…"

There was this young lad, Tim, who became a millionaire before he was thirty. Well, as the story goes, after finishing his O Levels, he could not go for further studies owing to lack of financial support, and had to work to sustain himself. He jumped from one job to another, but was never satisfied with his earnings. He wanted to make big money, quickly. But with no special skills, he knew he could not get far.

He had a very caring aunt who always advised him to do some studies through a night college, but he hated part-time studies. 'I wish there was a course which could be finished off quickly, and enabled one to earn big money,' he would say.

One day his aunt won a fortune on football pools. She told him:

"I really want more than ever to see you do some further studies, Tim. Choose a full-time course and I will pay for it. In fact, give you all the financial support you may need during your studies. You can pay me back when you start working after you are qualified. Okay?'

Tim liked the idea, but was not sure what studies he should do. Someone had once told him about a special computer course on industrial systems which, he learned, not only lasted a few weeks, it also enabled one to earn a good salary after one had done it. 'That is the sort of thing I would like to do,' Tim said to himself. The course fee, however, was astronomical—1500 a day! He talked to his aunt. She told him to go ahead.

Tim soon completed the course and secured a very good position with a large firm. This was just a start. Within a few years he became one of the top earners, owing to the shortage of people with his particular skill.

But the burning desire to make real big money, and to achieve complete financial freedom, had not left him. He started saving as much as he could. Within next five years, he had given up working for others, and started his own consulting firm.

The business really took off. There was only one other firm which offered similar services at the time, and it was large and financially stronger than his. To eliminate the competition from Tim's firm, they offered to buy it out. The price was more than what Tim had bargained for—a few million dollars in cash, plus a share in the business. They also offered him a bonus: a large luxury villa somewhere in California.

Tim accepted the offer. And who wouldn't? Retiring as a millionaire at the age of twenty-seven, to lounge in the sun, surrounded by all the luxuries one needs, is not a small deal.

"I guess," said Tim to one of his close friends once, "any ordinary person can become a millionaire. The secret lies in doing the right thing , at the right time, and at the right place, or TTP in short. Discover this golden combination in your life, and you are there."

Case Number 3

"Give them what they like best, and they will make you rich"

Michael was working as a bus driver for a transport firm in London when I first met him three years ago. He still does, but there is a difference. He no longer lives in a rented flat, but in a beautiful villa of his own. Did he get a substantial rise in his salary, or perhaps, win a lottery of some kind?

"No," he said, when I asked him, "I have a side business."

"A side business?" I remarked. "I thought you were fully occupied with your driving job."

"I am," he said with a smile, "but I also make some money on the side, sometimes more in a month than my pay as a bus driver."

On being prodded, he said: "Well, it is not something which could surprise you. I sell three piece suites."

"You mean you have a shop somewhere?" I asked.

"Sort of," he said. "Actually I work from home. Come I will show you."

He took me to the back of his house where he unlocked the door of a large wooden shed. As we walked in, I was amazed. The place was full of beautiful sofas.

"Oh, I see. So this is your shop." I said. "Who do you sell these to?"

"Ask me how do I sell them," he said. "Come on."

We returned to his drawing room where he picked up a local newspaper. Flipping through the pages, he stopped at the advertising section, and pointed at a 2" by 2" box advertisement which read:

"LUXURY AT LOW LOW PRICE. THREE PIECE SUITES FOR SALE. PLEASE HURRY. CALL…"

A telephone number followed.

"Are you making good money?" I asked.

"You want to know all the secrets, don't you?" he said, smiling. "Okay, I will tell you. Last year I made about 8000. I expect to make more this year. And apart from this, I also make about 200 a week in my present job."

"Your margin must be very low."

"No", it is about forty percent"

"And how can you manage that?" I asked.

"Ha ha," he laughed, "there lies the whole secret, the real thrill of the game. I get them from factories up North. Some can be classed as 'seconds' but you cannot tell the difference unless you examined them very closely. Still, they are new, and my customers know what they are paying for."

"There must be others around here who would be selling from home like you." I said.

"There are," he said, "but not in my line of business, since not everyone gets an idea of doing business from home; or it is just that many people do not know the 'where and how' of it. A fellow I know sells carpets from home. The secret is in finding a source where you can buy cheap, and sell, at a price, which should be reasonably lower than that charged by the big stores. Good advertising does the rest.

"When people know you are offering a reasonable quality at a bargain price, why should they go elsewhere. Remember, its the people who really count in business. Give them what they like best, and they will make you rich."

Case Number 4

"If you have them, then wealth is just around the corner"

John and Peter, two ordinary labourers in their late twenties, worked five good years for a builder. Today they are their own bosses and own properties worth 1,000,000.

One evening, they invited me for a dinner in a posh hotel in the city. While we enjoyed the good food, they unfolded their success story to me.

"Well," said Peter, "it all starts with ambition and drive. So did we. As it were, we became fed up working for the builder. It was real hard work with low pay. We always wished we were our own bosses. Since we did not have much formal education, getting a well-paid job was out of question. It took us five long years to realise, that we had to do something about our future. The general employment situation wasn't also good in those days, so quitting our jobs would have been a disaster. Self-employment was the only answer.

"Anyway, it all started when we jointly bought a house. We got it for 70,000, well below the market value, since it needed some doing up. Actually, it had belonged to a deceased lady, and her trustees were very eager to dispose it off quickly, as it was lying vacant for almost a year. Of course, we obtained a mortgage on it, almost 90 percent.

"Working late in the evenings and over week-ends, we completely renovated it. We also put a large extension at the back. It took us six months. It really looked superb after we had finished. The house market was going through a boom, so we put it up for sale. The first person who came to view it paid the asking price. We made straight 20,000 profit. We danced with joy at making so much money in such a short time. It really changed our whole thinking about money.

"We bought another similar property at a very much reduced price. This one was a corner property, and had a large plot of land on the side.

We obtained planning permission from the local council to build a two-bedroom extension on it. A finance company was too glad to advance us the money for the project. The extension was completed within eight months, and after completely renovating the rest of the property, we sold it during the peak summer time. Don't ask me how much we made on it. We almost doubled the capital we had invested in it.

"That venture really started the ball rolling. We quit our jobs and devoted full time to buying properties, and selling them after renovating or extending them. We also bought from auctions. Six years of hard work has brought us a long way. But we enjoyed every minute of it. Today we have our own building firm."

"We own a few properties around town," said John. "They are valued at just over 1,000,000."

"I often look back," said Peter, "and remember the hard days when we were just ordinary labourers. We never thought we would ever be rich, but today we know we are. It all seems like a beautiful dream. We have our holidays twice a year, and have visited most of the famous places in the world. And I am looking forward to an African safari on my next break."

"Our experience has taught us one thing," said John, "and that is, that one doesn't need to be too clever to make big money. It is just a matter of spotting the opportunities and using them; and most importantly, the drive to forge ahead, plus a little bit of confidence in oneself. Those are the ingredients you need to make a success of your life. If you have them, then wealth is just around the corner."

Case Number 5

"Wish we had thought of this earlier..."

When I first met Ken, he was working as an ordinary Parts Salesman with a firm of car dealers. About eight months later, when I saw him again, he was running his own business, buying and selling second-hand fridge's, gas cookers and other small electrical items. His shop was on a busy high street.

"How come?" I asked him.

"Well," he said, looking very happy and relaxed, "I was sort of forced into business. For ten years, I slogged as a salesman for the dealer. Despite working very hard, I couldn't save much. Nearing my forties, and a family to look after, I thought I wasn't going to get anywhere if things continued that way.

"The employment situation was also bad in those days. I hadn't had much further education, so there was little chance of finding a good job. To make matters worse, a new boss had taken over our department. He was harsh and a real mean person. Later, I learned, that he wanted to get rid of me to bring in one of his close friends. Started playing politics with me, you know. Realising that he was looking for an excuse to sack me, and that getting another job would be difficult, I started thinking of self-employment.

"I talked to friends and people who were in business, seeking advice. I gathered whatever information I could get from various sources on options available. I also visited Ted, an old friend of mine who lives up in Yorkshire. He is in big business, dealing in fridges and gas cookers, mostly factory rejects. He usually buys them in large lots and sells them to various shops round the country. He also reconditions old ones. He would have anything like two hundred units in his warehouse at anytime.

"Ted had always advised me to go for self-employment. 'You will make lot of money I tell you,' he would say, but I had never thought about it seriously. 'Find a shop in your town and I will supply you fridges, on very preferential terms,' he would often say. Think it over, at least before you lose your job!'

"So I thought it over, seriously this time. I discussed the whole thing with Sid, a close friend of mine. Sid had been on the dole for quite a spell.

He jumped at the idea of going into business and becoming his own boss. 'Why not?' he said.

"We soon started looking for a vacant shop in earnest. Luckily, we found this one, at 60 a week. The Enterprise Allowance we are getting is enough to cover our rent and rates. There is also a flat upstairs which we have let to a student attending a nearby university.

"Peter and I contributed 500 each. Our bank lent us a thousand. We bought a second-hand van for 700, spent a couple of hundreds on fittings and tools, ordered some fridges from Ted, and put an advert in the local paper. We were in business sooner than we realised.

"You would not believe it. We sold three fridges in the very first week, and made 200 profit. We jumped with delight at earning our first business income."

"Most of our customers are local landlords who let properties to university staff and students," said Sid.

"How much are you averaging net per week?" I asked.

"Well, about 500, I would imagine," said Ken.

"That must be better than your pay as a Parts Salesman," said I.

"It certainly is," said Ken. "We made more during last summer. The gas cookers also go well. We have also started stocking some new items like electric heaters, fans, domestic irons and toasters."

"Well," said Sid, "we have been in it for almost a year now. I have experienced one thing, though. And that is, that you never get the taste of real money until you have a business of your own."

"We take time off work whenever we want," said Ken. "I am buying a house of my own soon. I can afford some comforts now, you know."

"No more dole money or fear of losing a job now," said Sid.

"And no more bossing around," said Ken. "We are very happy and relaxed. Wish we had thought of this earlier."

"Better late than never," Said Sid, and we all laughed.

Case Number 6

"Once you are in the swing of things, you will never look back"

Chris and Nick, two close friends, had been unemployed for over a year. They lived in a shared flat in a London suburb.

"It really surprises me," said Chris to his pal one day, "how can he afford such expensive cars."

He was talking about one of his elderly neighbours. "He drives a Jag one day and a Rolls the next. And always the latest models. He must be rolling in money!"

"Well, why don't we ask him," said Nick. "Perhaps he has some magic formula which could rub on us. You are not going to drive that twelve-year old Mini of yours all your life. Are you?"

"How could you ask him about his business affairs?" said Chris.

"Well he appears to be a nice person to me," said Nick. "And since he must have made enough, he wouldn't mind giving poor guys like us a few golden hints."

"Okay, I will try," Chris said.

After a month, when Nick saw Chris again, the latter looked very jubilant.

"I managed to find an excuse to see him," he said. "He told me all about it. A real jolly good fellow he is, I would say."

"Out with it then," said Nick, impatiently.

This is what Chris's rich neighbour told him:

"You do not need special skills to become rich, son, as some people would imagine. Just a right, positive attitude of mind and alertness to opportunities around you. You have asked me how I do it. This shows your own positive attitude to know and learn; and that is your first step towards success.

"Well, as we all know, for most people the most common way of earning a living is to work for someone for a fixed pay. Don't blame them. They are brought up to think and act like that. But some are different, like me, who really hate to work for others and tied to a fixed routine. I like to be in control of my own time—time to think about things, and to look for opportunities. You cannot do that if you are tied to 9 to 5 routine, and spending your energies in making money for others.

"I had a steady job once. I was a store-keeper with a local firm. It went bust. Whole ten years of service down the drain. Times were bad then. I mean job-wise. However, I managed to get a job—as a forecourt attendant at a petrol station. The owner also dealt in second-hand cars.

"The work was below my standard, of course. I was getting far less money than what I made in my previous job. However, it turned out to be a blessing in disguise. I happened to discover, that the owner made most of his money in his car business. I came to learn a lot about the trade, the whole wheeling and dealing of it.

"I quit the job after a year. I had some powerful ideas up my sleeve. Guess what? I started dealing in second-hand cars myself. But in a small way. I had only 800 cash when I started.

"I bought my first second-hand car from an auction, and sold it the following week, after spending some money on it. Boy, I made 200 profit. It was the easiest money I had ever made in my life.

"The things really started changing for me from then onwards. Full of confidence, I forged ahead with my one-man car business. In the beginning, I used to travel up and down the country to get my cars. I would buy a car say, in Glasgow and sell it off in London the following week for a quick profit.

"A time came when I started going for the expensive models. In the beginning, I worked from home. Today I own a couple of showrooms rooms round town.

"I would say second-hand car dealing is, definitely, a live and thriving business, any time of the year. You can always make good money in it on regular basis, once you have learned the tricks of the trade. Anyone with some initiative can do it.

"My advice is: go for the popular models only, and start with the price range everyone can afford. You eventually learn to spot the best deals as you get into the thick of the trade.

"I used to buy from whatever source I could. Auctions, dismantlers, insurance and finance companies. Buy those which require least repairs. Avoid writeoffs. Sometimes you can get very good bargains from certain dealers, especially, on the cars repossessed under the H.P. agreements.

"Selling your cars is simple. Just place an advertisement in your local newspaper, or in the weekly advertisers like the Exchange and Mart and the Auto Trader. If you are dealing in expensive types, advertise them in some serious national newspaper, like The Times. You can sell to friends, to start with. You can also import and export them. On the Continent, for example, certain models cost less than similar models sold in the U.K., even after paying for the import duty. Most people may not know that.

"In this business you can start at any level. As I said, go for the cheaper models, until you have enough cash to deal in the expensive types. That way there is low risk, and also enables you to acquire experience of the trade as you go along. Once you are in the swing of things, you will never look back."

Case Number 7

"Making the move here was a real blessing"

Richard, a truck driver, lived in London for ten years until he decided to move to Birmingham. I asked him the reason.

"I had had enough," he said. "I just wanted an easy life. Wanted to get away from the traffic-congested roads and most importantly, the high cost of living there. I realised that I needed to earn more and more to support the family. Usually worked extra hours to make the ends meet. The stress was too much to bear. I was fed up of the whole environment. Anyway, my frustration came to an end when I discussed my problems with Felix, a friend of mine who lived in Coventry.

"'Your house must be worth a fortune,' he said. 'Why don't you sell it and move North. Say somewhere in The Midlands. I am sure after paying off your outstanding mortgage, you will have enough to buy two large properties there. Why not settle in Birmingham? It is the next largest city after London and property prices are almost half of those in the South. You can buy a big shop there for far less money than in London, but having an equivalent turnover, you know.'

"Felix had a point. The discussion with him put a new spirit into me, enabling me to rethink my position and to formulate a plan for the future. Yes, the property prices had really rocketed in the last few years. And my house was worth almost five times the price I had paid for it ten years back. The rise, in fact, had given me lifetime savings. Being an ordinary truck driver, I could not have saved half that amount, even if I had worked whole my life.

"'I must make best use of this heaven-sent capital locked in my house,' I said to myself. So, after carefully weighing the odds, I sold the property and moved to Birmingham.

"There was so much going on out there. It is completely a different city from the one I had visited ten years ago. The improved road systems and the National Exhibition Centre has given a new look and prestige to it. And unlike London, it takes only a few minutes to get out of town, and into the surrounding countryside, which is really beautiful.

"I bought two large adjacent properties, not too far from the city. Paid hard cash for them. I converted them into a Bed and Breakfast, keeping the lower portion of one for my own family. The income from it is very good. In fact, it is enough for me to live on comfortably for the rest of my life.

"Many people, in fact, have moved from the South into The Midlands, and further North, in the last couple of years. Most have used the cash realised from the sale of their properties in the South to good advantage, enabling them to afford an easy, stress-free life, away from the big cities. Anyway, as far as I am concerned, making the move here was a real blessing. I feel as if I have really started living again."

Case Number 8

"Its good money with less hassle"

Henry, an immigrant to this country, bought a sub-post office in South East of England in early seventies when he settled there. He ran it for some ten years, until he decided to make a move, looking for a change. Moreover, he was nearing his fifties, and wanted to do a business which could give him big income with less hassle. So he started looking for the right opportunity.

He travelled up and down the country, meeting various people who were in business. He discovered, from the information he had gathered, that although there were many types of businesses one could go for, a nursing home was the ideal one which suited his whims.

His mind made up, he started hunting for one. He learned more and more about the nature of the business, obtaining information on it from various sources. He made contacts with the estate agents who specialised in them, requesting details on ones which were on sale. He also read Dalton's Weekly and other magazines which advertised businesses for sale.

From his research, he discovered, that the asking price for most of them was out of his range, especially, of those located in the South. 'To buy one which would fit my budget, and also be large enough to produce good income, I would have to move towards North, where properties are less dearer,' he thought to himself.

After viewing some nursing homes around Midlands, he was still undecided. 'Perhaps, I should find a suitable property and convert it,' he said to himself. 'That way I could get away with a smaller outlay.'

During one of his viewing trips to the North West of England, he stumbled on an old two-storey building, sitting in a beautiful countryside village. It was an old maternity hospital, lying derelict for some years. 'An ideal thing,' he thought. 'Would cost at least 200,000 in the South. Henry got it for 40,000! This also included a three-bedroom villa standing a few yards from the main building.

Henry sold his sub-post office for 110,000—almost ten times the price he had paid for it. Armed with the capital, he moved with his family to their new home.

Henry converted the old hospital into a beautiful nursing home. It took him six months, and cost about him about 25,000. After the local council had approved it, he soon got it running in full swing.

When I visited him recently, he took me round to show the place. It was a large building, surrounded by neatly-mowed lawns, bordered by orchards of fruit trees.

"I could never have imagined that you would be running a nursing home one day," I said, laughing.

He laughed too and said: "I had been planning for something like this for a long time, you know. I worked really hard to get the place in shipshape. There are forty rooms, fully occupied at present. A team of some twenty staff run the place, including three qualified nurses, headed by a matron."

"How much do you make a year?" I asked.

"Well, as you know, DHSS pays me. I get anything from 150 to 200 a week for each occupant."

"With forty rooms, fully occupied, you must be grossing up some half million a year."

"About 350,000, to be precise," said Henry. "There is roughly, a forty percent margin in this type of business."

"Wow! That's great," said I.

"Yes, it is good money with less hassle," said Henry, returning a greeting from a pretty nurse who walked past us, as we strolled along the corridor on the first floor.

"It sure is," I said. "What do you do all day, then? I mean when you got all this staff to run the place."

"I play golf on most days. My wife actually looks after the place. Occasionally, I pop into a nearby town to get supplies. Otherwise, I just maw the lawn and do some gardening."

Later, sipping hot coffee in his drawing room, I asked him:

"Have you got any future plans?"

"The future is always there for anyone who aspires for it," he said. Yes, I have plans. In fact, I have already put one into operation. I am selling this place."

"Selling it!" said I, surprised. "With all the income and easy life it is giving you."

"It's not that. I have bought another property. A real big one. It is an old mansion near Leeds. And I am going to convert it into a nursing home. It will give me almost double the income I get from this one."

"That's great," I said. "How much are you selling this one for?"

"Let someone give me half million quid and I will quit."

"You are really forging ahead towards becoming a millionaire, Henry."

"You got to," he said. "Once you are in the money-making game, you get used to aiming higher and higher. And that's what makes it really exciting."

Case Number 9

"Keep looking for an opportunity in earnest..."

Very often, a change of place heralds a new beginning, bringing success, happiness and wealth.

Take for example Martin. I first met him in Uganda, East Africa, when I used to work there some twenty years ago. He was an ordinary car mechanic, who had been forced to leave school on premature death of his father, a year before he was due to take his O' Level exams. When I met him, he was working as self-employed at a petrol station, belonging to one of late father's close friends.

I had almost forgotten all about him, after I had returned to England, until I met him again by chance, when, during a holiday in California, I drove into a gasoline service station, located along a highway passing through a beautiful beach town.

As I joined the queue of limousines and flashy sports cars, waiting their turn to be served, I took stock of my surroundings. Sun-drenched, the place bustled with activity. The station office had an adjoining garage where some mechanics were busy repairing cars, raised on a couple of hydraulic ramps. A few yards away to the right, was a liquor store. Busy shoppers of all ages, including young girls clad in hot pants or bikinis, darted in and out of the store. The station was actually situated on a rise which offered a scenic view of the blue Pacific below.

A young, amber-haired guy soon attended to me. He filled up the tank, checked the oil and cleaned the windscreen. "Have a good day," he said when I paid him. And as I was going to drive out of the station, my eyes fell on someone who had emerged from the station office just then. "Martin!" I said to myself. "It can't be."

But it was him, all right. I swung the car round and parked it on one side. As I walked towards him, he also saw me and froze for a moment. Then a big "Hi" from him, and we rushed towards each other.

"You son of a gun!" he said in a typical American accent, as we shook hands and laughed.

"Nice to see you again," said I. "What are you doing here? Don't tell me you own the place."

"I do," he said. "Come on, let us sit in my office."

As we entered the office, he pulled out a couple of cans of root beer from a vending machine and handed one to me. As we enjoyed the cool drink, he told me how he had ended up in the States.

"You remember the turmoil in Uganda in 1972, when Idi Amin ordered out the British Asians. Well, I had thought of hanging around for a while, but the threat of an army terrorising the country, forced me to leave. Almost penniless, I ended up in the States.

"I went straight to Iowa, to stay with Jimmy, an American friend I had met in Uganda. He had always invited me to come to USA. He lives with his parents. A really nice family it is. His father, in fact, employed me in his auto workshop, while applying for my green card.

"I enjoyed my stay with them, but found it a little tough during winters, especially, when I was born and brought up in the warm, Equatorial Africa. So, after couple of years, when I had saved some money, I decided to make a move. I ended up in California.

"I bought a car as soon as I arrived here, and drove around to get the feel of the place, and also, to look for some kind of job.

"One day I drove into this service station, and immediately fell in love with it. 'Wish I could own a place like this,' I said to myself. Mac, the station boss, turned out to be a real nice guy. He informed me, that there was a general shortage of good mechanics in the area, especially, those who could repair foreign cars.

"'I think I have come to the right place,' I thought to myself.

"Mac offered me a job straight away when I told him all about myself. However, I struck a different kind of deal with him. And that was, that I would work on my own as self-employed, and repair foreign cars only. And for using his workshop facilities, I would pay him a third of whatever I earned. He gladly agreed.

"Boy, I started making real money within weeks. This new opportunity put a new life into me. Other local garages also sought my services at times. I did some short courses to refresh my skills, and also obtained a certificate, authorising me to test vehicles, like MOT in the U.K.

"Eventually, I also started dealing in second-hand cars, especially, the Japanese sporty types. This is a very affluent area, you see. People pay you well for the job. Some famous Hollywood celebrities also live around here.

"Mac was really pleased with the way things were going. After a couple of years, he offered me a partnership in the business. That was the luckiest break of my life.

"We pulled a lot of business together. Another three years, and having a swollen bank balance, I decided to buy the station outright. Mac accepted my offer, as he had been planning to make a move himself for some time."

"You are damned lucky, Martin." said I.

"You could say that," he said, laughing. "And from then onwards," he continued, "things really got better and better. Within another couple of years, I bought another service station a few miles from here."

"How much are you making a year, if I dare ask?"

"About quarter million dollars, all paid. The business itself is worth around $3,000,000. I have used my money wisely and invested most of it in properties."

"That's really great," Said I, marvelling at his success.

"I still remember the times when I was slogging whole day, just to earn what I pay to one of my pump boys today. But I have learned one thing. And that is, that if you keep looking for an opportunity in earnest, you will find it one day."

"Do you miss Africa?" I asked.

"I did," he said, smiling, "but in the beginning only. Actually, I visit Kenya every year. In fact, I have seen more of it now then when I used to live there."

Then looking at his watch, he said, "Oh, it's lunch time. Care to join me?"

"You bet. I would certainly."

"Come on then. There is a lovely open air restaurant down near the beach. I simply love their seafood."

THE 'CONCRETE' PATHWAYS

If you wish to assess a person's wealth, ask him how many properties he owns. Everyone wants to own something, but a wise money-maker would, usually, make property ownership his ultimate goal, as it is the real and 'concrete' pathway to big money and financial security. A difficult goal to achieve, but not completely out of reach, if one plays one's cards right.

Ordinary people have made big fortunes from simple property deals. Some make thousands almost overnight. You too can, if you knew a few secrets behind the scenes. The fact is, if you can own at least one property, then you can easily own another and another...and so on.

Presented below are results of some personal interviews, held with people who have been in the property game for some time. We hope, their experiences would prove to be very informative, and perhaps, inspire YOU to make a 'kill' in the property 'jungle' one day.

Case 1

"I bought an ordinary small family house first, put an extension at the back, and sold it within six months. I was richer by 20,000.

"This enabled me to buy a larger one. This one had a side garage, which I converted into a living room. I also put a room in the loft. When I sold the property after fifteen months, I made a capital profit of 50,000, which enabled me to go for a still larger property.

"I have changed five properties in the last ten years. It was rather inconvenient moving around, but today I live in a large luxury villa in a posh area of London. And no mortgages to pay!"

Case 2

"I usually buy a freehold property having a vacant shop on the ground floor with living quarters on the upper floors. I convert the shop into an Off Licence, or a sumptuous restaurant and then put it up for sale. Or sometimes, I let it out on a lease. This brings me a lump sum which I use, either to settle part of the loan on the building, or as a down payment for acquiring another similar property.

"I convert the upper floors into self-contained studios, and let them out to working tenants. The rent from the studios and the shop is sufficient to meet the repayments of loan on the property, and often, leaves me some cash to enjoy. I have been six years in this business, and ten times richer than when I first started.

"The value of properties I own today, is just over 1,000,000. I hope, with the property market on the rise, it will double in next five years."

"Property seems to me, the only way by which an ordinary person can become rich. But to succeed in it, you got to have knowledge of the market. Not only that, you must know what is going on around you. For example, you should ask yourself following questions, when you want to deal in property:

- Is there some new development taking place in the area?
- Are they building a new rail or road link to a certain town?
- Has the government approved a scheme to build a new shopping plaza in a particular district?
- Is there general shortage of properties in the area, for instance, due to full employment?

An influx of immigrants into a country, for example, can dramatically shoot up the price of properties generally. Remember the exodus of Asians from East Africa in the seventies.

Also, the expected lifting of trade barriers between countries in the Common Market, in 1992, could bring another round of sudden rise in the property prices, followed by another one, when Hong Kong was handed over to the Chinese a few years ago."

Case 3

"I am an ordinary factory worker. I had saved some money over the years to buy a dream house of my own. While hunting for one, I came to discover, that one of my co-worker had bought a house from an auction. 'If he can, I can,' I said to myself.

"The building society I was saving with, refused to advance me the full amount for a house I was going to buy from an auction. I talked to my bank manager. He agreed to advance me the balance, provided I paid him back within five years.

"So, I went and bought a house from an auction. It was in a bad state, but I got it for thirty percent less than the price of similar-sized properties in the area.

"Helped by a friend of mine, I completely renovated it. Within a year, it's price had shot up by twenty percent. I realised that I would be making some 40,000 profit if I sold it then. And I did. I could not describe my joy at making so much money in such a short time. It was like winning a lottery.

"Soon I bought another property from an auction. Lured by the taste of making big money, I continued to buy properties from auctions, and sold them after renovating them. The capital I built up thus enabled be to buy my dream house in the end, plus a business of my own.

"Property, I discovered, is the positive way to big money and financial independence, provided you know how to go about it. And buying from an auction is an ideal way to start.

"Most big auctioneers print a catalogue which gives details of properties which were to be auctioned at some future date. Just phone them to request a copy."

Case 4

"I started alone first. I bought a plot of land and built a flat on it, which I sold within a year. I made straight 30,000 on it. Later, I joined forces with two of my close friends who liked my ideas. Today we are in big business. We buy development land and build residential flats on it.

"Financing is never a problem. A merchant bank lends us the money—about eighty percent of the value of properties completed at each stage.

"We buy any property which will make money. For example, we buy old country hotels, which we sell off after renovating them to modern standards. We also buy empty plots of land near shopping areas and convert them into parking lots. We derive good income from them. If we get a good price, we sell them off.

"Recently, we bought a development land from a city council. We are building some thirty flats on it. The project would cost 2,000,000 over the two years' completion period. The eventual sale of these flats would realise 1,500,000 net, to be shared equally among the three of us."

Case 5

"I worked in various jobs over the years, but never made real money, until I went into business. I did various types: groceries, newspaper shops, restaurants. Within a period of ten years, I had about four shops running. But it was hard work.

"Eventually, I realised that the only way to make big money with less hassle, was via property. I gradually acquired the knowledge and inside secrets of the property market. The hottest areas, I learned, are the big cities, especially, where commercial properties are concerned.

"I bought properties and sold them after keeping them for a year or two, during which time, I would let them out. I built up a large equity that way. This enabled me to obtain substantial overdraft facilities from my bankers.

"I frequently buy from auctions. Often, after I had bought a property from an auction, I sold it the following month for a handsome profit, without even doing anything to it. I made thousands that way. Today, I own twenty properties round town, valued at some 2,000,000.

"Recently, I bought a block of flats in New York from an auction there, for $1,000,000. Most of the flats were already let when I bought the building. The rental income is not only sufficient to meet the repayments of loan I obtained to purchase the property, it also leaves me some cash to play with.

"My main advantage is my good reputation with my bank. In fact, I deal direct with the bank director now, not his juniors. I have agreed an overdraft limit of up to 2,000,000 with him. This enables me to snap quick deals at any time. When I see a property which suits my needs, I do not have to wait for a mortgage or loan. I just write out a cheque and get it."

A READY ROUTE TO BUSINESS WEALTH

There are people who yearn to go into business, but lack the courage to do so, or perhaps, may not have the know-how or experience of the business world. The formidable task of building a business from scratch, and the attendant risk of failure, deters many from taking the plunge. Some would, however, feel happy to run a business if it can be set up for them. Franchising could offer an opening for such people, enabling them to realise their dream of owning a business—a ready-made business.

Franchising is not something new. It is very common in the U.S.A., and has, only recently, gained popularity in other countries, including the U.K.

McDonald's Hamburgers, Kentucky Fried Chicken and Kall-Kwik Printing are some of the typical examples of a franchised business.

What actually is franchising then? It is simply a right to use the name and the know-how of an established business. It consists of a contract between the franchiser i.e. the owner of the franchise and, the franchisee, to whom the business is franchised.

A franchise contract can be of various types. But usually, it involves the franchiser agreeing to provide a 'ready-made' business to the franchisee. It may include the name, the know-how and the actual setting-up of the business. The franchiser would also provide administrative support, which may include training of franchisee's staff. In return, the franchisee agrees to pay the franchiser an initial fee, plus a share of the business transacted, usually a fixed percentage of his gross annual turnover. The contract is usually for a five year term.

The advantages of a franchise to both parties are obvious: the franchisee gains a ready-made business; the franchiser achieves wide distribution of his products or services at lower cost, since the risk is transferred

71

to the franchisee. The public also benefits from ready availability of a standard, high quality product or service that has been nationally or internationally accepted.

Franchising may have some disadvantages, though, but not many. The main one is the rigid nature of the business. You are not allowed to change the management style or image of the business. You may also have contractual obligation to purchase materials, products or ingredients from the franchiser, at a cost set by him.

Despite the pitfalls, franchising is a quicker method of entry into the business world, provided you have the necessary capital required to purchase the franchise. The initial fee could range anything from 5,000 to 50,000 and upwards, depending on the nature of business you are going for. Famous franchises like McDonald's may command a very high fee.

A list of commonly available franchises is presented for your guidance in Appendix III. Perhaps there is one which you may wish to go for. It could change your life and bring you prosperity.

FINDING MILLION PLUS CUSTOMERS CHEAP AND EASY

If you had a shop, you can only sell your goods if the people knew what were you selling, usually by visiting your shop. But how many would you expect to walk in and look at goods, displayed in your showroom? May be a few everyday, or a few hundred a week? And that means, your sale will be limited by those who actually visit your shop and buy the goods. Of course, you would wish more and more people would come and buy your goods. But that is only possible and practical, if you were in real big business.

However, in many business nowadays—unless it is a food store—it is not necessary for customers to actually visit the shop. Goods can be advertised and sold by mail order. The advertising media can range from your local newspaper to national one, or it could be a magazine, radio, or television. By advertising in any of these media, you could reach a few hundred to a few million prospective customers, depending on the media you choose. However, the more widely read a newspaper or magazine is, the more costly it is to advertisement in it.

Would you spend, say $40,000 on advertising every week ? Certainly not, unless you were a large organisation, like Johnson and Johnson. A full page advertisement in a popular tabloid newspaper in U.K., would cost just that—$40,000 plus. Although by spending that kind of money you could grab the attention of say, 5 million readers, you dare not spend that kind of money, unless you were sure that you could attract enough orders every time. A small, one man business, for instance, would seldom afford to spend that kind of money on advertising.

But nevertheless, however small a business is, it would always wish to have as many customers as possible. Don't you wish, if you were in business, that millions of people could see your advertisement, without your having to pay such an enormous price for it? Who wouldn't? Well, there is a way. And you too can use it. Anyone can use it today. It is the magic word of today's business communication—The Internet.

You can advertise your goods or services on the Internet at a fraction of the cost of advertising in any other media, and still, reach millions of prospective customers—50,000,000 plus and, increasing day by day. Imagine you are advertising a product on the Internet on which you intend to make, say a net profit of only $1.00 per unit sold. If just 1 % of the viewers ordered it, how much profit would you make? 50,000,000 x $1.00 x 1% = $500,000.00 just at one go! And how much would it cost you? Only $500.00—$1200.00—for a whole year's appearance on it!

This is a classical example of how opportunities can appear in different shapes, at different times, as discussed earlier. So why don't you use it? It could turn out to be your golden route to a million dollar fortune.

CASH AND WEALTH WITHOUT SWEAT

If you asked a business man, or some one with a special skills: "Can you give me a small share of your wealth or earnings?" Will he do it? Of course not. On the contrary, he might be offended, and probably reply: "Bugger off!"

Why should someone give you part of his earnings—even a fraction of it—unless, you were very close to him. It sounds highly improbable. But if you were to do something which promised some financial benefit to him, he would be more happy to co-operate with you.

You may say, "Well I don't have any special skills, so how can I be of any benefit to any business man, or some one with special skills?" You can. That is the point. You know, that any successful business man, or a highly skilled person, can often command good earnings, especially, if the latter is also in business. So, you can use their skills and resources to earn a big income yourself.

"How?" you may ask. Well, you know, at least, that a business man, whether skilled or not, is selling something—goods or services—to earn his income. And to be able to sell, he must find customers or clients , without whom he would not make any money. Agreed? Okay. Now let us take an example.

Suppose you know a lawyer, or say, a finance broker. If you talked to him, he will be most willing to pay you something, call it a commission, if you introduced clients to him. Now imagine, you knew five such business people with different skills e. g. a lawyer, an accountant, a financial broker, a large builder, and an estate agent. Suppose each agrees to pay you $200 fee for each customer introduced by you. Let us say, you introduced only 5 customers during your first month to just one of those professionals. You would have made straight $200x5 = $1,000. Over the year it would

75

be $12 000. And if you introduced 5 customers to each of them, you would make $60,000 a year! And that, without possessing any special skills yourself or using your capital.

"Now, how am I going to find so many customers?" you may wonder. And this is where you have to look around, and find out who needs what, as explained in an earlier chapter, i.e. you make money by identifying the needs of people and then satisfying those needs, by using skills and resources of others, without spending a penny of yours. Here you become, what we would call, a 'Zero-Zero Agent' i.e. one who starts with zero capital or expense; and can be an agent of anyone who wishes to buy something, and at the same time, an agent of anyone who wishes to sell something; you can get your cut either from the seller, or from the buyer, or even both like a 'double agent', and that, without ever working as a full time employee for either of them; you simply match the needs and wants of one against the skill and resources of the other.

But again, you might argue, "$60,000 is not enough for me. I wish to make a real fortune." Well, just find more buyers/sellers combinations, and you could steadily build up a fortune. But yet again, you might say, "I wish to make a real big 'kill' in the shortest possible time." But of course, you can. Simply go for the high value international deals.

For example, find a some one who wishes to buy say, 100 million dollar worth of some product or service, and also, some one who can supply it. In such deals, the agent, the intermediary, or the mandate—you could be in any one of those categories—gets a commission based on the value of the deal. The only 'hard' work you have to do is to bring the buyers and the sellers together, often through plain introduction, either directly, or through some private or business contacts. If the buyer agreed, under the $100 million deal, to pay you a straight commission of 1/2% of the value of the transaction i.e. of 100 million dollars, then you would end up making a clean $500,000—almost overnight! And if you arranged a few more deals like these over a year say, you would definitely be a millionaire! Wouldn't you? And that, without much sweat.

Of course, it may sound a bit difficult to find such big deals, but not impossible. Everyone knows some one who, through a chain of contacts, can reach a buyer who needs something, and a supplier who can supply it. On conclusion of the deal, they all can then share in the 'loot' which can run into millions of dollars.

There are many such deals going around internationally, all the time. Most of these relate to commodities, e.g. crude oil and, even some hard currencies like the New Kuwaiti Dinars. Mostly large quantities are dealt with—$50 million to a few $billion. The important thing is to find a supplier willing to supply at a discounted price i.e. at a price which is lower than the ruling market price, and a buyer who can buy at that price. The latter often pays the commission involved, to both the seller's agents and the buyer's agents or intermediaries for getting him a good deal. Examples of such deals include trades involving:

- Sugar—100,000 metric tons per month over say 12 months.
- Crude Oil—2 million barrels a month over say two years.
- Currency—1 billion Kuwaiti Dinars exchanged against US dollars.
- Construction project—say 50 million dollars worth.

Multi-million dollar fortunes are being made almost everyday, by ordinary, but 'clever' people around the globe, from many such deals, sometimes, by just acting as intermediaries between the seller and buyer 'groups'. You too can do it, without a big effort on your part. The only 'tool' or 'skill' you need, to get into the 'thick' of such deals, is simply the awareness of:

1. What is going on around you and internationally, and
2. Who are responsible for making high level buying and selling decisions in businesses i.e. contacts.

And how do you acquire that awareness? Simply follow the 'Pathways' explained earlier. They are your golden keys to success, and will lead you automatically to the threshold of opportunities—opportunities which will make you a millionaire, without working for someone whole your life.

THE CHOICE IS YOURS

Whether you wish to make extra cash on regular basis, or make money in a big way, the choice is yours. There are scores of business ideas one can think of and try. May be you already have something in mind. However, to enable you to make some kind of a start, we have prepared a list of some current business ideas and opportunities which you may like to have a go at. The list is shown in Appendix II.

You may notice from the list, that many businesses could be started without much capital, or without carrying huge stocks of goods. Some of them can even be operated from home. Please also remember, that an idea could be used in many different ways. In fact, many people have made big fortunes by adapting some old ideas to current business trends. Once an idea appeals to the public at large, it is a winner.

The best way to embark on the road to riches is to do the following:
- Read the guide again, slowly this time. Consider the 'pathways' open to you.
- Look at the business ideas or opportunities listed in Appendix II. Make a short-list of those which interest you most.
- Examine each in turn. Gather more information about them if required.
- Select one which appears most suited to your particular aims, ambitions and financial circumstances.
- Draw up a plan of action.
- Proceed to give practical effect to your plan.

Remember action makes it all happen. So what are you waiting for?
JUST GET THE BALL ROLLING !

APPENDIX I
BUSINESS EVALUATION

The following form can be used to plan/evaluate a business you may wish to acquire. It can be modified, if required, to suit different situations. The answer column, for instance, can be extended to include separate sheets containing detailed information.

Business Evaluation Questionnaire

Question	Answer

A-The Nature of Business
1. What type of business am I looking for?
2. What price range am I looking for?
3. My preferred locations (state country, town, area, etc.)
4. Property details:
   - Do I want a freehold or leasehold?
   - Do I want to rent the premises?

B-The Actual Business (when located)
1. The value of the business:
   - What is the asking price?
   - Is it a fair valuation of the business?
     (examine the audited accounts)
   - If a leasehold property, the term of the lease?
   - Are the assets stated at correct values?
   - Is the goodwill asked for reasonable?

2. Financing of the business:
   - How much total capital do I need?
   - How much capital do I have?
   - How much can I borrow?
   - Where am I going to borrow from?
   - What will be the rate of interest?
   - What will be the period of loan?
   - What are other start-up costs?

3. The operating efficiency of the business:
   - What is the turnover?
   - Has it increased/decreased over the years?
   - How much is the gross margin?
   - Is it normal for this kind of business?
   - How much is the net profit?
   - What are the major expenses/costs?
   - What is the return on capital employed?
   - Is it reasonable/good/excellent?

4. General questions:
   - What is the competition like? (generally/locally)
   - Who are the major customers?
   - Is the trade seasonal?
   - Is there room for more expansion?
   - Who are the major suppliers to the business?
   - Are they reliable?
   - Are the staff required readily available?
   - Is the business subject to some strict legal requirements?
   - Are there any major developments taking place in the area?
   - Would they affect the business in any way?
   - Why is the owner selling the business?

C-Does the business really meet my personal and financial objectives?

FINAL DECISION
Purchase the Business?   YES / NO   DATE
Reasons:

APPENDIX II
LIST OF CURRENT BUSINESS IDEAS

- Car Maintenance
- Buying and selling second-hand cars
- Auto Tune Shop
- Car engine reconditioning
- Money from selling car number plates
- Vehicle rental service
- Television/Video Maintenance
- Refrigeration reconditioning/repairs
- Washing machine reconditioning/repairs
- Gas and electrical cookers reconditioning/repairs
- Double glazing
- Plumbing service
- Roof repairing
- Home decoration
- Carpentry service
- Home electrical wiring
- Furniture making
- Upholstery service
- Car velveting cushioning service
- Money from leather work
- Mobile locksmithing service
- Key cutting service
- Assembly work for factories
- Jewellery Assembly
- Doll Assembly

- Making lamp shades
- Toy making
- Carpet cleaning service
- Home/Apartment cleaning service
- Gardening service
- Rubbish clearance/skip service
- Garden Shed Tool and equipment hire
- Picture framing
- Flower making
- Photography
- Filming
- Painting
- Knitting
- Dress making, sewing, mending
- Shoe polishing
- Shoe repairs
- Baby sitting/child minding
- Private primary/secondary tuition
- Birthday cake making
- Mobile catering service
- Selling health and beauty care products
- Buying and selling second-hand furniture
- Dealing in antiques
- Selling unwanted clothes
- Car boot sales
- Art dealer
- Selling through market stalls
- Money from clearance sales
- Money from auction sales
- Delivery round and mobile shop
- Mini cab/taxi service
- Typing service

- Word processing service
- Accounting service
- C.V. Writing service
- Interpreting and translation service
- Computer bureau
- Computer hiring
- Computer programming service
- Computer training
- Internet Cafe
- Internet super store and other services
- Management consultancy
- Investment consultancy
- Mortgage/loans broking
- Insurance broking
- Credit and debt collection service
- Market research service
- Money from arranging contracts
- Business communication and address service
- Leaflet distribution service
- Selling for commission
- Selling books by mail
- Book binding
- Buying and selling old magazines/comics
- Mail order marketing
- Direct marketing service
- Money from selling lists (Names and Addresses)
- Buying and selling charts
- Writing for profit
- Money from selling information/ideas
- Mail order publishing
- Money from newsletters
- Pen friendship club

- Marriage bureau
- Dating and escort service
- Marriage counselling service
- Tuition for specific courses
- Martial arts instruction
- Hair saloon
- Massage parlour
- Body building/fitness centre
- Sports/leisure centre
- Health/swimming club
- Billiard halls
- Nursing home
- Retirement home
- Bed and Breakfast
- Fast food Take-aways
- Food restaurants
- Property buying and selling
- Industrial tools and equipment hiring
- Vehicle car park/storage
- Cold room storage
- Money from farms/animals
- Food supermarket
- Laundry/drycleaning service
- Sub-post office
- News agency
- Employment agency
- Estate agency
- Driving school
- Letting service
- Travel agency
- Video tape rental service
- Publishing a Newsletter

- Internet Services
- Web Design Services
- Internet Cafe Service

Franchise Opportunities

ACCOUNTING SERVICES
ADVENTURE PURSUITS
ANTIQUE RESTORATION
AMENITY WEED CONTROL
ALTERNATIVE MEDICINE
AQUATIC SUPPLIES
BATTERIES RETAIL AND WHOLESALE
BATH RENOVATION
BRICKWORK POINTING
BEDROOM FURNITURE
BEAUTY PRODUCTS/TREATMENT
BADGES-NAMEPLATES
BUSINESS SALES
COMPUTER SERVICES
CARPET RETAIL AND FITTING
CHIMNEY LINING/REPAIR
CLUTCH FITTING SERVICE
CHILDREN'S CLOTHING RETAIL
CURTAIN SERVICE/RETAIL
CARPET CLEANING/RENOVATION
COFFEE SUPPLIES AND SERVICE
CONVENIENCE STORES
CONFECTIONERY RETAIL
DOMESTIC CLEANING
DRAINS SERVICE

DAMP-PROOFING BUILDINGS
DRY CLEANING
DAIRY SUPPLIES/WHOLESALE/RETAIL
DOUBLE GLAZING
DOOR AND WINDOW FURNITURE
DESIGNER SHELVING SYSTEMS
DRESS JEWELLERY
DENTAL SUNDRIES/SUPPLIES
DISCOUNT AIRLINE TICKETS
EXHAUST REPLACEMENT SERVICE
ENGINE TUNING
ESTATE AGENTS
ENERGY CONSERVATION
ENGINEERING WORKSHOP SUPPLIES
EXHIBITION ORGANISERS
FOOTWEAR-RETAIL
FLOOR AND WALL APPLICATIONS
FREEZER PRODUCTS (FOOD)
FINANCIAL SERVICES
FITNESS STUDIOS
FRIED CHICKEN TAKE-AWAYS
FIREPLACES AND ACCESSORIES
FITTED KITCHENS
FURNITURE CARE AND RESTORATION
FORK LIFT TRUCKS
FOOD RETAIL AND BULK CONTAINERS
FLAME PROOFING AND RETARDANT TREATMENT
FRANCHISE SERVICES CONSULTANCY
GLASS ENGRAVING
GARAGE DOORS(REMOTE CONTROL)
GRAFFITI REMOVAL AND PROTECTION
GARDEN BUILDING AND ACCESSORIES

HAIR TREATMENT
HORTICULTURE SERVICES
HEALTH FOOD RETAILING
HOT BREAD KITCHENS
HIGH CLASS LINEN RETAIL
HOME CARE PRODUCTS-DIRECT SELLING
HOTELS
INSURANCE
INSURANCE SERVICES-PROPERTY
ICE CREAM-MOBILE AND STATIC SITES
INFORMATION SERVICES TO LEISURE INDUSTRY
INCENTIVE HOLIDAYS
INTERNATIONAL LICENSING
KNIFE MAINTENANCE SERVICE
KITCHEN SHOPS
LADIES FASHION WEAR
LEISUREWEAR-RETAIL
LUXURY CHOCOLATES
MARINE SUPPLIES AND SERVICES
MENSWEAR HIRE AND RETAIL
MEXICAN FAST FOOD
MOBILE TOOLS-RETAIL
MEDIA MARKETING
MOBILE FIXINGS AND FASTENER SERVICES
MOBILE LUBRICATION UNITS
NURSING SERVICES
NATURAL COSMETIC PRODUCTS
OFFICE AND COMMERCIAL CLEANING
PERSONNEL SELECTION AND PLACEMENT
PUBLICATIONS MERCHANDISING
PASTA PRODUCTS
PHOTOGRAPHY SERVICES

PIZZA RESTAURANTS
PRINT SHOPS
PLUMBING SERVICES
PARCEL DELIVERY SERVICES
PICTURE FRAMING SHOPS
PAINT STRIPPING SERVICE
PROPERTY CONVEYANCING
PERFUME AND TOILETRIES RETAIL
PROPERTY RENOVATION
PET AND LIVESTOCK FOOD SUPPLIES
POSTERS, PICTURES AND PRINT SELLING
PROMOTIONAL SERVICES
PERSONALISED EMBROIDERY SERVICE
PLASTIC REPAIR SERVICE
ROAD REPAIR SERVICE
READY MIXED CONCRETE
REPLACEMENT WINDOW AND DOOR RETAILING
RETAIL FOOD VAN SALES
RADIATOR SALES AND REPAIR SERVICE
RESTAURANTS-FULL SERVICE
SECURITY SERVICES
SIGNS SUPPLIERS
STAINED GLASS SERVICE
SOFT DRINK WHOLESALE/RETAIL
STOCKTAKING AUDITS
SEWING/KNITTING MACHINES SALES AND SERVICE
SPECTACLES RETAILERS
TRAVEL AGENTS
TRAINING FACILITIES
TAXI SERVICE
TOOL HIRE
TIMBER PRESERVATION

TIES AND SCARVES SALES
TENT AND MARQUEE HIRE
TELECOMMUNICATION EQUIPMENT
TACHOGRAPH ANALYSIS SERVICE
TYRE RE-TREADING
THATCHING SERVICE
VEHICLE VELVETING
VETERINARY SERVICE
VIDEO SUPPLIES AND SERVICE
VEHICLE COMPONENT MOBILE SALES
VACUUM CLEANER SERVICES
VINYL REPAIRS
VEHICLE HIRE/RENTAL
VEHICLE ALARM SERVICE
VACUUM SYSTEM INSTALLERS
VEHICLE LEASING FINANCIAL SERVICES
VIDEO LEASING/SALES
VIDEO RECORDING SERVICE
WINDSCREEN REPAIR/REPLACEMENT
WEDDING/BRIDAL WEAR/HIRE
WINDOW BLINDS RETAILING
WATER SPORTS
WAR GAMES
YOGURT RETAIL SALES

APPENDIX III
USEFUL INFORMATION SOURCES

There are many international sources of information which could be useful to an aspiring money maker. Public libraries could be an excellent starting point for obtaining them. They could give one ready access to publications which give detailed information on many important, national and international organisations, concerned with helping business-minded people. The following sources are some of the important ones, and may serve as a guide to the type of information one could find useful.

Useful Addresses

- Alliance of Small Firms and Self-Employed People, 42 Vine Road, East Moseley, Surrey. KT8 9LF. Telephone 0181-979-2293
- British Franchise Association(BFA), 75a Bell Street, Henley-on-Thames, Oxon RG9 2BD. Telephone 01491-578049
- Commission for New Towns, Glen House, Stag Place, London SWIE 5AJ. Telephone 0181-828-7722
- Companies Registration Office, Companies House, 55 City Road, London EC1Y 1BB. Telephone 0171-253-9393
- Small Firms Division, Department of Trade and Industry, Ashdown house, 123 Victoria Street, London SW1E 6RB, Telephone 01-215-5544
- Small Business Bureau, 32 Smith Square, London, SW1P 3HH Telephone 0181-222-9000

- The Department of Environment, 2 Marsham Street, London SW1P 3EB. Telephone 0181-212-7158
- The VAT Central Unit, Alexander House, 21 Victoria Street, Southend-on-Sea SS99 1AA. Telephone 01702-348944

Some Property Auctioneers (International)

Name	Country	elephone
Sallman Harman Healy	London	01-405-3581
Properties At Auction	New York	212-319-8550
Goddard & Smith, Int'l	London	01-930-7321
Arthur Lloyd	Paris	45 63 09 90
Studio Maggi	Milano	86 19 41
Richard Stanton Pty. Ltd.	Sydney	231-6611
Goddard & Smith Int'l	Dublin	680 466
Properties At Auction	Toronto	366-4975
Goddard & Smith Realty Ltd.	Vancouver	683-7535

Some Organisations Who Buy/Promote Inventions

International Product Design, 1-7 Harley Street, London, W1N 1DA, England Tel: 0171 436 1127

Inventions To Industry Ltd., Portman House, George Street, Aylesbury, Bucks, HP20 2HU. England. Tel: (01296) 84141

Some Important Business Publications

Fortune

Time, Inc., Time & Life Building, 1271 Avenue of the Americas, New York, N.Y. 10020 U.S.A.

Income Opportunities

Davies Publications, Inc., 380 Lexington Avenue, New York, N.Y. 10017 U.S.A.

Money

Time, Inc., Time & Life Building, Rockefeller Centre, New York, N.Y. 10020 U.S.A.

Travel & Leisure

American Express Pub. Co., 1350 Avenue of the Americas, New York, N.Y. 10019 U.S.A.

World Trade Digest

Wade World Trade Ltd., Wade House, Queen Street, Swindon, Wiltshire SN1 1RJ England.

Business Opportunities Digest

Institute Of Small Business, 11 Bloomfield Street, London, EC2M 7AY England.

Streetwise Business

Lincoln House 661 High Road London N12 ODZ England.

Business Opportunity World

Merlin Publications Ltd FREEPOST (BR1155) Hove BN3 6BR

PC Magazines

A variety of them available at any good news shops

IMPORTANT NOTES

www.ingramcontent.com/pod-product-compliance
Lightning Source LLC
Chambersburg PA
CBHW030851180526
45163CB00004B/1533